"*Learning Humility* is Richard Foster's pilgrim journey seeking and showing the way of humility. This tender, gentle retelling weaves the wisdom of the Lakota peoples and the humble way of Christ and his followers to reveal a stirring vision of humility. In our day of overheated egos and endless self-fixation, Foster offers us the cool water of deeper connection found through humility. In the midst of our confusion, he shows the slow and welcome process of clarity found through humility. This is the book I've been looking for, and I will return to it over and over, continuing to learn this humble way that my soul longs for."

Lacy Finn Borgo, author of *Spiritual Conversations with Children* and *All Will Be Well: Learning to Trust God's Love*

"In the way that the world was given the four agreements through Don Miguel Ruiz's Toltec lens, Richard Foster offers a vibrant and refreshing new view using the lens of the Native North American Lakota people. We need a diverse lens. I celebrate the discipline Richard undertook of his year-long experiment with *Learning Humility*. I am grateful for the welcoming language that gives a new way of seeing and humbly being open to living our most expansive with-God lives. Richard's is a fresh word for our times and a deeply soul-satisfying reminder of this virtue so desperately needed."

Juanita Campbell Rasmus, spiritual director and author of *Learning to Be*

"Humility is an essential and highly nuanced topic for us Christians; there are such fine lines to be found—between humility and humiliation, self-regard and self-promotion, healthy self-esteem and the sin of pride. Foster finds the line and walks it beautifully. The idea that we do not try to attain humility directly but we 'come at the matter indirectly. We simply take up those things that, in God's time and in God's way, will lead us into the virtue of humility' is tremendously hopeful. It is worth the price of the book."

Ruth Haley Barton, founder of the Transforming Center and author of *Sacred Rhythms*

"Destined to be another classic from Richard J. Foster, *Learning Humility* is a gift from a gifted writer. In this book we get to walk with Richard not only on the trails of Colorado but also on the terrain of the soul. Richard is a true scribe of the kingdom who brings forth treasures old and new (Matthew 13:52). The breadth and depth of the wisdom bearers he quotes is immense, from Peter and Paul, to Evagrius and Julian, to Chief Joseph and Underhill, to Kelly and Law, and to Murray and contemporary writers. Framed by the thirteen months and moons of the Lakota and filled with liturgies and litanies, this book ignited in me a hunger for humility in my own life. This is one of Richard's signature gifts: he makes us long for difficult things by helping us see that virtues, like humility, are the pearl of great price, worth giving all we have to obtain it. This book is an engaging and insightful gem, and I am the better for having read it."

James Bryan Smith, author of *The Good and Beautiful God*

"Richard Foster shows how humility is not a confusing burden of trying to be something we'll never be but a way of being that focuses on God's goodness and results in being naturally kind, free of striving, and more lighthearted. Don't miss it!"

Jan Johnson, author of *Abundant Simplicity* and president of Dallas Willard Ministries

"In his latest book, *Learning Humility*, Richard Foster opens up the pages of his journal and grants us access to his yearlong 'prayer experiment' of cultivating this foundational—and countercultural—Christian virtue. With winsome candor and the unassuming posture of a learner, Foster wonders, wrestles, seeks, confesses, and puts into practice ways of cooperating with the Holy Spirit's work of transformation. As he notices and names his own temptations toward pride, he gently holds up the mirror for us to notice and name ours as well. A seasoned mentor, Foster reminds us to keep pace with the slow, lifelong work of grace while not neglecting our call to embrace and embody the cruciform, humble way of Jesus. This is a challenging, thoughtful, soul-stretching book."

Sharon Garlough Brown, author of the Sensible Shoes Series and *Feathers of Hope*

RICHARD J.
FOSTER

Learning

Humility

A YEAR OF SEARCHING
FOR A VANISHING
VIRTUE

An imprint of InterVarsity Press
Downers Grove, Illinois

InterVarsity Press
P.O. Box 1400 | Downers Grove, IL 60515-1426
ivpress.com | email@ivpress.com

InterVarsity Press® is the publishing division of InterVarsity Christian Fellowship/USA®. For more information, visit intervarsity.org.

Scripture quotations, unless otherwise noted, are from the New Revised Standard Version Bible, copyright © 1989 National Council of the Churches of Christ in the United States of America. Used by permission. All rights reserved worldwide.

While any stories in this book are true, some names and identifying information may have been changed to protect the privacy of individuals.

The publisher cannot verify the accuracy or functionality of website URLs used in this book beyond the date of publication.

Cover design and image composite: David Fassett
Interior design: Daniel van Loon

ISBN 978-1-5140-0212-4 (print) | ISBN 978-1-5140-0213-1 (digital)

Printed in the United States of America ∞

Library of Congress Cataloging-in-Publication Data
A catalog record for this book is available from the Library of Congress.

29   28   27   26   25   24   23   22 | 8   7   6   5   4   3   2   1

To Carolynn, my heart,

We met for the first time fifty-six years ago and in that first
meeting you stole my heart. I have never regretted the theft.
Over these many years we have been through thick and thin, ups
and downs. Sometimes we were taken where we did not want
to go . . . especially so through The Cancer Years.
But we faced it all, both the good and the bad, together.

I dedicated my first book, Celebration of Discipline, *to you. Now,*
for this book (which might well be my last), I also dedicate it to you.
I love you, dear Carolynn . . . more than words can ever tell.
Yours for eternity,

—Richard

Contents

A Beginning Word

NEW YEAR'S EVE—A DIVINE NUDGE

Tonight I have been meditating on New Year's resolutions, wondering if I need to undertake any for this next year. Actually, I dislike these attempts at self-improvement. For the most part they are simply humanly initiated efforts that usually last about two and a half weeks. Still, while I was holding the idea before myself, I sensed a nudge . . . perhaps a divine nudge. It came to me in two words: "learn humility."

Hmm. I wonder, *Should I give this next year to see what I can learn about humility by study and by experience?* Both the Bible and the devotional masters give high priority to this virtue.

Yet it is a virtue that is not thought much of today.

Perhaps I could follow the calendar year and then maybe I can keep a journal record of my observations and musings. I'm not particularly good at journal writing . . . I probably have a dozen half-written journals sitting over there on my bookshelves. Still, I'd like to see how things develop here.

NEW YEAR'S DAY—THE LAKOTA CALENDAR

Thoughts about writing on the subject of humility keep pressing in on me. If I am going to use the calendar year as the organizing principle for this project, I think I would prefer to use one of the Native American calendars rather than using the traditional names for the months . . . January, February, etc. Their intentional rootedness in the natural world is a welcome departure from the scattered, patchwork nature of today's social rhythms.

All of the Native American calendars have their merits; however, I like the Lakota Moon Calendar best, especially its close connection to the earth. There are two differences between the Latin/Gregorian and the Lakota calendars to be aware of. The most obvious difference is that the Lakota calendar is divided into thirteen moons (of twenty-eight days) rather than the twelve months we are acquainted with in the Latin/Gregorian calendar. Hence, there is a rough (though not exact) correspondence to the months most of us would recognize. Second, the Lakota calendar (like most Native American calendars) begins with spring since spring symbolizes the start of a new year through the birth of new plant and animal life. Instead, I will begin with winter and "The Hard Moon," which roughly corresponds to January in the Latin/Gregorian calendar. This is when the idea of studying the topic of humility first came to me.

The Lakota are the northern plains people, and, while a part of my personal background is Ojibwa (my paternal grandmother, who died before I was born, was Native American—Ojibwa; also called Chippewa, self-named Anishinaabe), I find the Lakota calendar most attractive to me. Perhaps learning more about the culture that gave rise to it will yield some interesting insights. The reverence in Native American cultures for creation contrasts with a contemporary culture that presumes it can engineer human society to achieve more and better.

PART I

The Cold and Dark Moons

(WINTER—*WANIYETU*)

The Hard Moon

JANUARY 1–28

*Take my yoke upon you, and learn from me; for I am gentle
and humble in heart, and you will find rest for your souls.*

JESUS (MATTHEW 11:29)

*Because Christ had thus humbled Himself before God, and
God was ever before Him, He found it possible to humble
Himself before men too, and to be the Servant of all.*

ANDREW MURRAY

《 《 《 《 《 FIRST WEEK 》 》 》 》 》

AN INHERENT CONTRADICTION?

It is a beautiful cold morning and the meteorologist says it is supposed to snow throughout the day. So, I build a warm fire and
decide I'm in for the day.

By now it's mid-afternoon and I know that Carolynn will be
nervous about leaving the mail in the mailbox overnight; mail theft
is a real possibility in our rural area. If I collect the mail now Carolynn will rest easier tonight. Our mailbox is half a mile down the
road and with this snow (fully seven inches now and well on its way
to ten, maybe twelve) driving will be difficult. Thus, I decide to walk
down and secure the mail. Besides, I am wondering if this little task
just might be a small act of humility for me. I layer my clothes, take
my trekking poles, and set out.

The road is quite deserted of cars—plow trucks have yet to come through. After collecting the mail I decide to leave the road and make my way back home through the woods. This route is more difficult. The snow is wetter and deeper than I thought and I am wishing I had worn my snowshoes.

The stillness of the woods allows me to meditate a bit on my humility project. I realize these journals could one day become public. Writing on this particular topic while knowing that others might someday read it carries with it an inherent danger . . . perhaps an inherent contradiction. I think I'll just hold the matter before the Lord for now.

READING SLOWLY

Today *The Cloud of Unknowing* comes to mind. I think I remember two or three chapters in it devoted to the subject of humility. I'll look them up and see what I can learn. With *The Cloud* I will need to take it exceedingly slow, sitting with any one passage for an extended time. In my past excursions into *The Cloud* I have tended to breeze through a section and afterward walk away confused. Or worse yet, I would arrogantly assume that the book has nothing to teach me. So, I need to remember that here slow, slow, slow is the way forward.

THE SUPREME TOUCHSTONE

Biblical passages on humility abound, but the supreme touchstone has to be the example of Jesus. Paul describes it so wonderfully that it is best quoted in full:

> Let the same mind be in you that was in Christ Jesus,
>> who, though he was in the form of God,
>>> did not regard equality with God
>>> as something to be exploited,
>> but emptied himself,

taking the form of a slave,
being born in human likeness.
And being found in human form,
he *humbled* himself
and became obedient to the point of death—
even death on a cross. (Phil 2:5-8)

Once we begin thinking of Jesus as the touchstone for an understanding of humility we see that everything is there.

- Strength. Courage. Competence.
- No domination. No self-centered arrogance. No easy pushover.

THE DIVINE PARADIGM

By meditating on Jesus' life we see humility take on flesh and blood.

- A humble birth in an obscure village.
- The growing-up years in quiet obscurity.
- Magnificent teachings to "the sat upon, the spat upon, the ratted on."
- The Twelve chosen without regard to position or status or title.
- The wonder-filled miracles that did indeed draw enormous attention. And note carefully how Jesus handles all this fame without manipulation, without control, without domination.
- The borrowed donkey for his entry into Jerusalem; the borrowed room for his Last Supper.
- The disciplined silence throughout a mock trial and conviction.
- The enormous courage of suffering for the sins of the whole world. This has to be the supreme example of humility.
- The cry of abandonment, "*Eli, Eli, lema sabachthani*, My God, My God, why have you forsaken me?"
- The cry of humble triumph, "It is finished."

As I look at this all it begins to dawn on me that Jesus is indeed the divine paradigm for conjugating all the verbs of humility.

I'm also reading along in the many other Scripture passages on humility. So much to ponder—wow! I'm beginning to think I will need to take a private retreat in order to soak more completely in the biblical witness.

(((((SECOND WEEK)))))

This Little Act of Loving

I found the pertinent section on humility from *The Cloud*. There are three key chapters—thirteen, fourteen, and fifteen. I think I will stay with them for a week or so and see what I learn. Here is a statement I especially like which connects loving contemplation to humility. I found it in chapter twenty-five: "As I said before, this little act of loving called contemplation mysteriously contains humility and charity, as well as all the other virtues." I'll need to sit with this one for a while.

Struck by Three Things

Coming back to *The Cloud* after several years away from it I am immediately struck by three things.

First, I am struck by the refreshing beauty of a non-self-promoting author. Today it seems that an author's writing skills or whether they actually have something to say are far less important than the size of the author's platform, how popularity can be increased, and how much coverage the author can garner. On and on *ad nauseam*. *The Cloud*'s language reveals an articulate and engaging author. But, while scholars have worked hard to discover the identity of this author, all efforts have failed. I rather imagine this is just the way our anonymous author wanted it.

I have no answer to our contemporary dilemma. But I am refreshed by the author's complete freedom from human praise. Perhaps his/her personal obscurity is an important teaching in itself . . . teaching us that Christ should be the focus of attention and his followers become more unassuming, more kind, more humble. How would this teaching play in our narcissistic culture?

Second, I am struck by how dynamic and contemporary the message of *The Cloud* feels. The one specific detail we do know about this book is that our anonymous author is writing to a twenty-four-year-old who is also anonymous to us. Talk about speaking to the heart needs of Millennials! Here is a resource par excellence for the twenty-something person who wants to move beyond the superficialities of modern culture.

Third, I am struck by the gentle wisdom found in *The Cloud*. This is true for the entire volume, and never more so than when the author touches on the topic of humility. I wonder, *What is the connection between wisdom and humility?* I don't know, I just wonder. I'd like to tease this out in the days ahead.

(((((THIRD WEEK)))))

The Awful Rust of Sin

The Cloud's guidance on humility is imminently practical and filled with pastoral care. It begins with the simple yet profound definition: "humility is seeing yourself as you really are. It's that simple." And I concur, "Yes, it is that simple."

The word *humility* comes from the Latin *humilitas,* meaning "grounded" or "from the earth." Think of our word *humus* (earth, soil). Hence, with humility we are brought back to earth. We don't think of ourselves higher than we should. Nor do we think of ourselves lower than we should. No pride or haughtiness. No self-deprecation or feelings of unworthiness. Just an accurate assessment of who we actually are. Our strengths and competencies. And, yes, our weaknesses and shortcomings.

And this is exactly where *The Cloud* turns our attention. We have no idea if our anonymous author had read Aristotle, but he (could our author be she?) clearly understands the value of self-knowledge. "Self-knowledge is the only way to get and keep the virtue of humility." *The Cloud* adds, "Don't flinch in the face of the tremendous work involved. Get to know yourself. Yes, it is backbreaking labor. Embrace it. Through it, you'll experience God as he is. I don't mean you'll know God completely. . . . But when you get to know yourself better as the mortal human you are, your soul grows in humility, and you'll know God as fully as possible on earth."

So, how do we experience this self-knowledge? *The Cloud* teaches that "self-reflection" is the best way for us to know ourselves as we truly are. In a posture of deep humility in itself our anonymous author states, "I will admit that those who sin on a regular basis (and I have and do) need this sort of self-reflection. We must be humbled by the memory of our sinfulness and past mistakes, until the awful rust of sin is scrubbed away."

Right alongside *The Cloud*'s stress on the importance of self-knowledge is the qualification that self-knowledge is "an imperfect humility." The author's point being that a focus on knowing the self as fully as possible still leaves us with a focus on the self.

The move from an "imperfect humility" to "perfect humility" comes as we are enabled by divine grace to turn from ourselves to God alone. The author writes, "The best way to grow in humility is not through reflecting on our weaknesses but by remembering

God's goodness and love. . . . 'Perfect' humility comes when you experience God's goodness and superabundant love."

Our anonymous author does add a sobering note. In this life "perfect humility" is a temporary, almost fleeting experience. It comes "when, by grace, you allow the hidden love of your pure heart to press against the dark cloud of unknowing between you and God." Even though our experience is "fleeting" our counselor/author speaks a word of encouragement: "I . . . want you to be able to recognize perfect humility so you can set it up in your heart as a sign of love. It becomes something to aim for. . . . I believe that the mere awareness of perfect humility will help you be more humble."

SØREN KIERKEGAARD

Somewhere in his *Journal* I remember Søren Kierkegaard writing, "Now, with God's help, I shall become myself." I rather think this fits quite nicely with the teaching of *The Cloud* on humility.

A SIMPLE PRAYER

A simple prayer has been drifting in and out of my consciousness in recent days. I haven't gotten the wording quite right and so decided that writing it out might help me articulate the inner yearnings.

> Loving Lord Jesus, I humbly ask that you would . . .
> Purify my heart,
> Renew my mind,
> Sanctify my imagination, and
> Enlarge my soul.
> Amen.

I think it would be good to stay with this prayer for a while.

THE HUMAN SIDE AND THE DIVINE SIDE

Took a hike today with my little prayer as my companion and sensed that there are two sides to its answer: the human side and the divine side.

On the human side

- With regard to *heart purity*, I am *to consider* tenderly the crucifixion of our Lord Jesus Christ. I am *to see* his heart as an open wound of love toward all humanity. And I am *to feel* the divine love pouring out of his wounded heart for me.

- With regard to a *renewed mind,* I am *to think* on whatever is true and honorable and just and pure and pleasing and commendable (Phil 4:8). Not all the time, but whenever I am able.

- With regard to a *sanctified imagination*, I am *to picture* the new heaven and the new earth, the new Jerusalem, the river of the water of life bright as crystal, and the tree of life on either side of the river whose leaves are for the healing of the nations (Rev 21–22). Imagine that! Picture this, not constantly, only as I can.

- With regard to an *enlarged soul,* I am *to find* people I can serve. In small ways, and even large ways. Whenever possible.

On the divine side

- With regard to *heart purity*, God alone purifies the heart. God alone will straighten out the twistedness of all desires. God alone will radiate light into every dark corner.

- With regard to a *renewed mind*, God alone will train the mind into deep habit patterns of righteousness and peace and joy in the Holy Spirit (Rom 14:17).

- With regard to a *sanctified imagination,* God alone slowly, slowly, slowly channels all the imaginings into that pure stream which is comprised of the good and the true and the beautiful.

- With regard to an *enlarged soul,* God alone will place deep within the subterranean chambers of the heart and the mind and the imagination an understanding of the overwhelming preciousness of every single person.

Then came this authoritative word: remember that God is . . .

- quick to forgive
- eager to heal
- glad to restore

(((((FOURTH WEEK)))))

My Search for Elena Ferrante

Right now I am reading an essay Lar gave me from *The Atlantic*: "My Search for Elena Ferrante." It is about an Italian pseudonymous author who goes to great lengths to hide her identity, maintaining only that her identity lies in her writing. Hmm. Does anonymity reflect an underlying humility?

Captivated My Mind

At the church service this morning I was immediately struck by the last stanza in the processional hymn, "O God, Our Help in Ages Past." The words captivated my mind and I heard little else. I decided that this stanza was what I needed to focus on at this time. It is a stanza that is omitted in the hymnbooks I have at home.

> Time like an ever-rolling stream,
> bears all our years away;
> they fly forgotten, as a dream
> dies at the op'ning day.

And what does this have to do with humility? Well, it most certainly puts all our "magnificent accomplishments" in their place! . . . "They fly forgotten, as a dream dies at the op'ning day."

THE LAKOTA VIRTUES

Since I am using the Lakota calendar to frame these journal entries, I thought it might be useful to consider Lakota cultural ideals as I go along. The twelve Lakota virtues create a nice frame for a year of reflection, one for each of the next twelve months.

They are

- Humility
- Perseverance
- Respect
- Honor
- Love
- Sacrifice

- Truth
- Compassion
- Bravery
- Fortitude
- Generosity
- Wisdom

The Moon When Trees Crack from the Cold

JANUARY 29–FEBRUARY 25

What does the LORD require of you but to do justice, and
to love kindness, and to walk humbly with your God?

MICAH 6:8

All the virtues are interconnected; the truly humble
man is also truthful and courageous.

BASIL PENNINGTON

(((((FIRST WEEK)))))

THE FIRST VIRTUE

The first of the twelve Lakota virtues is *Unsiiciyapi*, "humility."
Honest. I did not change the order; humility is the first virtue of the
twelve. Here are some comments about this virtue: "The first and
most important step in life and especially on the spiritual path is
humility which is the opposite of pride. In terms of spirituality, if
the step of humility is skipped it results in delusions of grandeur.
Humility is the foundation of all the other virtues. If you brag about
your generosity then it spoils the generosity."

I find these thoughts to be quite consistent with a Christian understanding of the moral life.

A Roaring Fire

It began snowing this morning and is supposed to continue all day and into the night. There is no sense in clearing a way out to the road until tomorrow, hence this is a good day for me to stay in and turn the time into a one-day retreat. Hopefully, this can allow me to dwell on some of the many biblical passages that deal with the theme of humility. A couple days ago I brought in a good stock of firewood in anticipation of the snow coming. So, I have built a roaring fire downstairs in my study and went upstairs to let Carolynn know that I am in retreat for the day. She is delighted to leave me alone so she can give her full attention to income tax matters (bless her).

The snow comes down in absolute silence. No wind whatsoever. This, of course, quiets everything out in the woods. Outside my study window I can see the deer scratching and grazing. A layer of snow covers their backs but they seem oblivious to it all. The temperature is supposed to drop down to zero as the evening comes on. I am quite cozy with my fire warming the entire downstairs. Just now I take a cup of coffee and sit in my chair, which faces the fire. The logs pop and crackle a bit but even these sounds seem subdued. I sit still until the coffee cup is empty, quietly considering various passages on humility and arrogance and related themes. I wonder . . . where does arrogance rear its ugly head in my life? How may I cultivate humility of heart more fully? Can I learn simply to do justice, to love mercy, and to walk humbly with God?

I end my retreat with my brain feeling fried and go to the treadmill for a little exercise. Today going out in the weather is not wise, though that is where I would rather be!

Two Special Words

A special word enters our New Testament from a vast background in Greek philosophical thought and tradition. The word is *aretē* and the normal English translation is "virtue." The apostle Peter, for example, uses *aretē* as he provides us with a progressive list of how we are to grow in grace: "add to your faith virtue (*aretē*); and to virtue knowledge; and to knowledge temperance; and to temperance patience; and to patience godliness; and to godliness brotherly kindness; and to brotherly kindness charity" (2 Pet 1:5-7 KJV).

Another word that enters our New Testament is *dikaiosynē* and it is often translated as "righteousness." In what we have come to call the Sermon on the Mount Jesus teaches us, "unless your righteousness (*dikaiosynē*) exceeds that of the scribes and Pharisees, you will never enter the kingdom of heaven" (Mt 5:20). Actually, both words mean the same thing: "to function well." Plato tended to use *dikaiosynē* and Aristotle used *aretē*. Aristotle won the linguistic battle and even today we speak of "virtue ethics" to describe efforts to understand ethical or virtuous behavior.

Now, this understanding of *aretē* meaning "to function well" is genuinely important for us today because we have become so accustomed to the normality of "dysfunction." Indeed, we can hardly even conceive of a person who functions well!

The concept of virtue was developed considerably in Greek thought, especially by Aristotle in his *Nicomachean Ethics*. Indeed Aristotle had an entire list of virtues. Interestingly, humility was not on his list.

THE PANTHEON OF VIRTUES

The idea that "humility" should be placed among the pantheon of virtues is deeply Hebraic and Christian in origin. In the Greek and Hellenistic world "humility" (*tapeinos* in Greek) was far from something to be valued, or even desired. Humility was almost universally used in a pejorative sense meaning "insignificant," "servile," "lowly." Gerhard Kittel, in his exhaustive *Theological Dictionary of the New*

Testament, writes, "The Greek view of humility exalts freedom and despises subjection. Hence it qualifies *tapeinos* negatively."

However, the life and teachings of Jesus place humility in an entirely different light. Jesus declares, "The greatest among you will be your servant. All who exalt themselves will be humbled, and all who humble themselves will be exalted" (Mt 23:11-12). And Paul in his magnificent hymn in Philippians 2 writes about the signal action of Jesus who humbled himself unto death, even death on a cross. The New Testament writers use *tapeinos* some thirty-four times, always with a positive ring.

Early Christian scholars took this radical rethinking of humility and classified it under the notion of *aretē,* virtue. John Cassian, for example, calls humility "the mother and mistress of all the virtues." He adds that, in contradistinction to the pagan understandings of virtue in his day, humility "is the precise and magnificent gift of the Savior."

Our contemporary culture views humility in much the same negative manner as the ancient Greek and Hellenistic world. So, the Christian witness to the enormous value of humility as a central virtue is just as countercultural today as it was in the first century.

(((((SECOND WEEK)))))

HUMILITY COMES FROM ELSEWHERE

Augustine of Hippo is the key theologian to insist on humility as a specifically Christian virtue. He explained that the other philo-sophical traditions of his day—Epicurean, Stoic, and Platonist—simply disregarded humility. Even the great Aristotle does not include humility in his list of virtues. Why? Well, Augustine's answer is simple: "Humility comes from elsewhere, from the One who, being the Most High, wished to empty Himself for us."

It is stunning to think that Christ, in his life and teachings, turned the human understanding about humility on its head. All the more important for we who seek to follow in his steps to value this central Christian virtue.

HUMILITY AND SERVICE

I will need to interact much more with the biblical witness, but already I am struck by the close connection between humility and service. Right after resolving a dispute among the Twelve over who is the greatest, Jesus states, "I am among you as one who serves" (Lk 22:27). And the wise apostle Paul writes, "For by the grace given to me I say to everyone among you not to think of yourself more highly than you ought to think, but to think with sober judgment, each according to the measure of faith that God has assigned" (Rom 12:3). With this as a backdrop Paul then launches into a teaching on how we are to live in unity: "We, who are many, are one body in Christ, and individually we are many members one of another" (Rom 12:5).

Anyway, this paring of humility and service feels like a helpful concept to consider. I think I shall experiment with it for a while and see what I can learn.

SERVICE AND ANGER DON'T MIX

Today I learned the hard lesson that service and anger don't mix. I was working in the kitchen cleaning this and that. Indeed, I was rather proud of my little act of service!

Just then Carolynn made a remark that did not sit well with me. I quickly responded in anger . . . and, of course, I got back exactly what I deserved. Our anger only lasted a short time and we quickly made up. But by this point any thoughts of humility were out the window.

It did underscore for me how destructive anger is to any genuine service. The incident helped to solidify in my mind how the virtues are all interrelated. Kindness, patience, gentleness, humility, service, and more; they all work in concert.

SERVICE WITH CHILDREN

I am seeing that service with children often needs to take the form of play. Not doing things for them or teaching them, but simply playing with them. Also, singing with little ones. I rather imagine that humility grows more easily in this environment because of the absence of pretense that we experience with children. Perhaps we can say that the lack of pretense purifies our actions of service.

THE COURAGE TO SERVE

Humility, I think, has a way of giving us the courage to serve. Courage. At first I thought the word I really wanted was *insight* or *wisdom* or even *strength*. But, no, *courage* is the word I am after. I often hesitate to serve out of a concern about what others may think about my act of service. Anyway, I think it is humility of spirit that at times infuses us with the courage to serve in good and life-giving ways.

(((((THIRD WEEK)))))

SERVICE AND MOTIVES

I think I am detecting a difference between acts of service that are done with mixed motives as opposed to service with more pure motives. Perhaps we could say, the purer the service the deeper the humility. Of course, we can never have completely pure motives about most anything. So, this is not something to fuss over. It is simply something to observe and step back from whenever the mixture of motives becomes too toxic.

A Critical Connection

In *The Rule of St. Benedict* we find his "twelve steps of humility." I'll plan to return to this material in due time, but right now I notice that many of these steps are working on service in one form or another. The focus is either on service to God or loving service to others in the community. So, even Benedict saw a critical connection between humility and service.

The Dance of the Snowflakes

It is snowing lightly this afternoon. The flakes are quite individualized falling from the sky. Actually they seem to be not so much "falling" as "dancing" as a frosty breeze tosses them hither and yon. The breeze appears to reverse the descent of some flakes tossing them up higher and then permitting them to descend. Others are twirled around and around on a downward spiral. Every flake will eventually come to rest on the ground covering the pine needles, but they do seem to be taking their time. In my home office I have pulled up all the shades so I have a completely unobstructed view through all four windows of the dance of the snowflakes among the trees. I have yet to build a fire as I was out on errands with Carolynn in the morning hoping to return before the snow came . . . and we have succeeded! Now I have the afternoon and evening unencumbered to watch patiently as the snow, with various detours, descends.

The devotional masters always taught us to read two books: the Bible and the Book of Nature. I wonder if the Book of Nature has anything to teach me about humility. I don't know, I'm just wondering.

(((((FOURTH WEEK)))))

I FELT AN EMPTINESS

I write this in the middle of the night because I can't sleep. In the afternoon we received the sad news of Bruce's death. Upon hearing it Carolynn wept a bit and I . . . well, I felt an emptiness the rest of the day.

I remember well when Bruce came to the university to teach psychology. We—Bruce and I—soon developed a collegial relationship, and Carolynn quickly fell into a close friendship with his wife, Judy.

Our relationship deepened when Bruce was hospitalized with a serious brain aneurysm. Together Carolynn and I went to the hospital to pray for him. Not just for comfort or peace but for total healing and complete restoration to normal functioning.

Now, over the years I have prayed with many dear folk for their healing. I have had to walk with some of them to the grave. Others have improved over time, though never fully. Still others have had rapid and relatively complete recovery. But Bruce's healing could only be described as miraculous. As we were praying it felt like the healing light of Jesus surrounded Bruce, and the aneurysm began dissolving as the body began restoring itself to health and well-being. Over all the years of ministry and prayer for physical healing I can count on one hand the number of "instantaneous" healings of this nature.

I think of Bruce and Judy as two of the most humble people Carolynn and I have ever had the opportunity to know. No strutting. No name dropping. No efforts to impress. No parading of academic credentials. It made them easy to be with.

Eventually they moved to Springfield, Illinois, so Bruce could take a professorship in their denominational seminary. Later they relocated to Urbana, Illinois. All through the years we have stayed in touch and visited each other. I loved the visit we had with them in Springfield, where Bruce showed me around all the Abraham Lincoln sites. Bruce was something of a lay historian in the field and so our tour included a running commentary on a multiplicity of intriguing and obscure details in the Lincoln story.

Over the years Bruce sent me a couple of books he had written in his chosen field of psychology. They were too technical for a general audience but I found them intriguing . . . at least the parts I could follow. (Our oldest son holds a PhD in clinical psychology, and I have the same difficulty with his writings.)

Tonight I consider Bruce and the way in which humility seemed to permeate him through and through. So many in his academic specialty seem entirely self-focused and arrogant. His loving service to others, most especially his students, and his complete personal self-forgetfulness were truly amazing. Knowing him has immeasurably enriched my life.

HUMILITY AND REPENTANCE

Tomorrow is the beginning of that season in the Christian calendar known as Lent . . . the forty days of preparation for the central event of our faith—the resurrection of Jesus, the Christ.

I've tended to have a rather dim view of the contemporary practices surrounding Lent. Often these practices are embarrassingly trivial . . . perhaps fasting from coffee or chocolate or other equally trite things. And for me the liturgical traditions that have grown up around Lent seem to be little more than efforts at "organized gloom," with no genuine rationale for the gloom. I'm often sorely tempted to tell earnest folk that for Lent I plan to fast from prayer. (And I confess that now and again I have yielded to this temptation.)

However, this season I am drawn to a particular practice found in the Eastern Orthodox Church, a practice that seeks to nurture an interior posture of "humility and repentance" for the Lenten season. (It was the characterization of "humility and repentance" that caught my attention.) Three weeks before Lent begins the Eastern Church observes "the Sunday of the Publican and the Pharisee." This, of course, is drawn from Jesus' well-known parable recorded in the Gospel of Luke (18:9-14).

Luke observes that this parable is specifically directed to those "who trusted in themselves that they were righteous and regarded others with contempt" (v. 9). Wow, is this ever an indictment of today's modern state of affairs . . . *trusting in ourselves that we are righteous and regarding others with contempt.* This is the very spirit that saturates the internet and floods talk radio and blogs without number.

In the parable the "prayer" of the Pharisee is far less a prayer than a self-righteous rant: "God, I thank you that I am not like other people: thieves, rogues, adulterers, or even like this tax collector. I fast twice a week; I give a tenth of all my income" (vv. 11-12). Then the contrast of the publican (a tax collector) could not be more striking. He stands far off, keeps his head down, beats his chest, and cries out, "God, be merciful to me, a sinner!" (v. 13). If we are searching for a model of profound humility, this is it.

This Lenten emphasis on "humility and repentance" keying off of Jesus' parable of the publican and the Pharisee feels worth exploring. So, I will give some thought to a fitting subject for a Lenten experience of humility and repentance.

The Moon of the Sore Eyes

FEBRUARY 26–MARCH 25

Now the man Moses was very humble,
more so than anyone else on the face of the earth.

NUMBERS 12:3

If anyone would like to acquire humility, I can, I think,
tell him the first step. The first step is to realize that one is proud.

C. S. LEWIS

(((((FIRST WEEK)))))

IN SPITE OF DIFFICULTIES

The second of the Lakota virtues is *Wowacintanka*, "perseverance." It is said of this virtue, "In spite of difficulties we persist in our efforts which is a deeply empowering source of strength rising from within. . . . Many of our ancestors were faced with challenges that could only be helped through spiritual strength. This perseverance was what carried them through even to the afterlife."

Even without the benefit of the full revelation we have in Jesus Christ these are instructive words. I'm glad to think on them.

A GOOD LENTEN EXPERIENCE

Today is Ash Wednesday, the beginning of Lent. I took a pass on the liturgical service where the pastor/priest places the sign of the cross in ash on the forehead. Not because I have anything against it. Indeed, I rather view it as one of the more meaningful rituals connected with Lent . . . it is a good reminder that we are dust and to dust we shall return. No, I passed on the service because I have yet to frame what might be a good Lenten experience of "humility and repentance" for me.

I have just begun reading *The Lakotas and the Black Hills* by Jeffrey Ostler. Perhaps it will help me find a right personal practice for me for Lent.

LENTEN MEDITATION 1—A PROPER SPIRIT

Okay, I feel clear to focus this Lenten season in "humility and repentance" on the blatant land grab of the Black Hills from the Lakota people in the mid-1800s, depriving them of many of their sacred sites such as Wind Cave, Devils Tower, and Bear Butte. I'll use *The Lakotas and the Black Hills* as a kind of devotional guide through Lent and see what I can learn. Most of all I'll need a prayer-filled inwardness to guide me through these forty days. Dear Lord, do lead me into a proper spirit of humility and repentance for atrocities of the past.

THE QUALITIES OF HUMILITY

I've noticed that it seems much more difficult to write about virtue than about vice. Think of the number of books written on one aspect or another of the seven deadly sins. How many books do we have on the virtues? A small number by comparison, I am sure. The same is true with film. It seems so much easier to explore the dark recesses of evil than it is to personify goodness. So, I'm thinking of devoting the next few weeks to seeing what I can do to explore some of the qualities of humility.

FREEDOM, JOY, AND HOLY HILARITY

Tonight I am reflecting on the distinguishing features of those who are characterized through and through by humility of heart. As I watch and consider such folk, three things always seem to stand out: freedom, joy, and holy hilarity.

Freedom. I'm thinking of things such as the freedom from always needing to speak up and straighten out everyone on this issue or on that matter. The freedom to be genuinely happy when others succeed. The freedom from the perennial urge to control or manage others.

Joy. I'm thinking of that deep, heart-felt joy in the goodness of God. Joy that the power of the Lord is over all. Joy that I can trust those I love in the care of God.

Holy hilarity. It seems to me that humble folk laugh a lot. Somehow they can easily see the comedy that the twists and turns of ordinary life bring us. Not the boisterous laughter that is at the expense of others. No, I mean joyful laughter at the quandaries that come to us almost daily. Laughing is the other side of weeping, and those soaked in humility are able to do both freely.

FREEDOM FROM DOMINATION AND CONTROL

I think one of the clearest signs of humility is a complete freedom from all domination and control. Humility has no desire and no need to force anything on anyone. Demanding is a posture foreign to a humble spirit. Humility possesses a friendly ease with others.

Humble folk seem to have almost an unconscious playfulness about them. My guess is that this is because they have no human reputation to protect and they are free from building a reputation for others to admire.

Loved for Her Beauty

Somewhere in my reading I came across the phrase, "Humility is loved for her beauty." I failed to note the source and now I cannot remember from whence it came! But I rather like it. Still, I wonder if it can be borne out in experience. Is this just a warm sentiment or is it empirically verifiable?

A Welcoming Kindness

As I watch humble people I find in them a welcoming kindness. They have no need to impress or show off or do anything that calls attention to themselves, hence they seem able to fully enjoy the presence of others. It is an inviting quality that I find quite pleasing. Indeed, every time I see it I long for this quality to be in me too.

I find it instructive to see how Paul links kindness and humility together with a host of other virtues: "As God's chosen ones, holy and beloved, clothe yourselves with compassion, kindness, humility, meekness, and patience. Bear with one another and, if anyone has a complaint against another, forgive each other; just as the Lord has forgiven you, so you also must forgive. Above all, clothe yourselves with love, which binds everything together in perfect harmony" (Col 3:12-14).

Wisdom Is with the Humble

Proverbs 11:2 says, "Wisdom is with the humble." A rather bold, flatfooted statement. Of course, this is characteristic of proverbs: they just come right out and say it, and then leave it up to us to test out the saying in life experience.

The Wisdom from Above

James 3:13 seems to second the motion made by the proverb: "Who is wise and understanding among you? Show by your good life that your works are done with gentleness born of wisdom." James goes on to teach us that "bitter envy" and "selfish ambition" are far removed from the wisdom of God. In summation he adds, "the wisdom from above is first pure, then peaceable, gentle, willing to yield, full of mercy and good fruits, without a trace of partiality or hypocrisy" (Jas 3:17). To my mind all this fits nicely with the spirit of humility.

No Embellishments, No Exaggerations

It seems that all the great virtues are connected in unseen ways: love, courage, duty, bravery, honor, and so much more. Humility, it seems, is right there among them. Humility appears to be especially important because it has no need to say more than what is actually the case. No embellishments. No exaggerations. No need for an oath to insure the truth. The humble person simply says what is actually the case, oath or no oath.

(((((THIRD WEEK)))))

Lenten Meditation 2—The Spirit of Greed

The Black Hills (Lakota *He Sápa*) is an isolated, five-thousand-square-mile, oval-shaped mountain range rising out of the Great Plains of North America. We know that it was the center of Lakota culture since at least 1776, and likely long before. In 1868 the US government signed the Fort Laramie Treaty, establishing the Great Sioux Reservation west of the Missouri River and securing the Black Hills for the Lakota people "forever" after earlier treaties had been broken. However, in 1874 George Armstrong Custer led an expedition into the Black Hills, resulting in the discovery of gold. Hence, in 1877 by an act of Congress the United States confiscated the Black Hills from the Lakota Nation.

The taking over of the Black Hills was an act of greed par excellence, the thirst for gold. How destructive, how evil is the spirit of greed. It was a horrendous act displacing an entire people. In my small way I repent of this grievous act.

As I do this I also need to search out the spirit of greed that hides in my own heart. Not greed for gold perhaps . . . maybe greed for the good reputation of another. Forgive me, Lord. Cleanse Thou my heart from the spirit of greed.

A FORCE OF CHARACTER

I'm beginning to wonder if humility possesses that essential "something" in an individual's personality which gives rise to a certain force of character. A force of character that is winsome and compelling, a force of character that stands out in contrast to all the hubris and babble that permeates the very air we breathe today.

THE FEELING TONES OF HUMILITY

I am wondering about the feeling tones of humility. Can we feel humility? Can we touch humility? Perhaps . . . with the fingers of faith.

AUTHENTIC CHRISTIAN COMMUNITY

Authentic Christian community is shaped by virtues that the world cannot grasp. And humility in particular is central for such community life to function.

This is especially critical for today when we are witnessing a shrinking moral vocabulary in public life. These thoughts draw me to Dallas Willard's final work, *The Disappearance of Moral Knowledge*. Are we slipping into a new dark age? I'm not sure. Regardless, one contribution we can make in these dark days is to create new expressions of Christian community life where a rich moral vocabulary can be preserved. Even more, we want to take such a vocabulary and incarnate it into the push and shove of daily life.

LENTEN MEDITATION 3—THE LOSS OF A WAY OF LIFE

Today the best-known site in the Black Hills is Mount Rushmore with the figures of George Washington, Thomas Jefferson, Theodore Roosevelt, and Abraham Lincoln carved into the granite.

The Lakota name for this magnificent granite bluff was *Thunkášila Šákpe*, "The Six Grandfathers." The name came from a vision of Lakota religious leader Nicolas Black Elk: "The vision was of the six sacred directions: west, east, north, south, above, and below. The directions were said to represent kindness and love, full of years and wisdom, like human grandfathers." For centuries the granite mountain remained carved only by the wind and the rain until 1927 when Gutzon Borglum began his blasting and chiseling work.

I am ambivalent about the Mount Rushmore site. I've been there and I understand the awe and patriotic feelings it aims to inspire. But I am also told that Lakota people coming to this site weep for the loss of a way of life. In my spirit I too weep for the loss of a way of life.

STRENGTH AND HUMILITY

Are the humble strong? Hmm. I wonder. The general culture often associates strength with aggressiveness, even ruthlessness. Is this a proper understanding of strength? I doubt it. Certainly firm convictions and humility work together in a kind of symbiotic relationship.

This leads me to think that I need to explore issues related to humility and leadership. But later. I'll want to read up on the subject some first . . . and most of all to ponder the matter more carefully.

HOMEY, EVERYDAY TASKS

I don't quite know how to describe the quality I am thinking of. I don't even know if it is a quality . . . maybe just a tendency. It seems like humility enables a person to undertake homey, everyday tasks more easily and with greater equanimity. I mean things like washing dishes or sweeping the floor. Things like mowing the lawn or changing baby diapers (for this one I had to reach way back into my memory banks!). And, if so, doesn't pride (humility's opposite) tend to make such ordinary tasks more burdensome? It seems so in my own experience.

(((((FOURTH WEEK)))))

A CHEERFUL, INTELLIGENT CHAP

I am helped by C. S. Lewis's description of humility:

> Do not imagine that if you meet a really humble man he will be what most people call "humble" nowadays: he will not be a sort of greasy, smarmy person, who is always telling you that, of course, he is nobody. Probably all you will think about him is that he seemed a cheerful, intelligent chap who took a real interest in what *you* said to *him*. If you do dislike him it will be because you feel a little *envious* of anyone who seems to enjoy life so easily. He will not be thinking about humility: he will not be thinking about himself at all.

What appeals to me here is how Lewis in a few carefully chosen words is able to give us such a vivid picture both of humility and its opposite, pride.

HUMILITY AND TRIUMPH

Yesterday the Gospel reading in church was John 20:19-29—the story of "doubting Thomas." I've always felt empathy with Thomas who, having missed out on the first appearance of the resurrected Christ to the gathered disciples, wanted empirical evidence: "Unless I see the mark of the nails in his hands, and put my finger in the mark of the nails and my hand in his side, I will not believe."

The next Sunday Thomas receives exactly what he needed. Jesus appears to the disciples a second time (even though the doors were bolted shut) and first says to the whole group, "Peace be with you." Then he turns to Thomas saying, "Put your finger here and see my hands. Reach out your hand and put it in my side. Do not doubt but believe." What an encounter! And dear Thomas, he responds with the stunned confession, "My Lord and my God!" Quite appropriate!

What I find thought provoking about the story is the unlikely combination of humility and triumph. Thomas was humbled, no doubt about it. He had asked for evidence and he sure got it. Yet he also ends up in triumph with a confession that would be fully accepted in any liturgical service in the world. Humility and triumph . . . I rather like the combination!

TENDING THE FIRE

A nice snow began this afternoon and according to the meteorologist it is expected to continue on through the night. Two days ago I hauled in a good store of wood in hopes of this eventuality. Since this is likely my last fire of the season, I decide to tend my fire all through the night, sleeping in the rocking chair facing the fireplace.

Two events from my past nudge me in this direction. The first occurred one winter when, as a boy of eight, I slept every night in a rollaway bed by the fireplace, our sole source of heat. That winter I become the tender of the fire, and to this day my memories of that time are deep and happy.

A second experience is tied to the time I helped our son Nate drive his van from Michigan to Florida. The van had been left with a friend in Michigan when Nate and family moved to Florida. It was now time to retrieve the van along with several boxes of leftover packing. Nate brought his son Kyren along, hence the three of us had a high, hilarious time all the way down to Florida. The experience was all the more memorable for a hole in the van's muffler which grew in size and sound as we made our way south, and we harbored some concern that the highway patrol just might pull us over!

By design the highlight of our trip was driving through the Great Smoky Mountains National Park. We paused to hike and marvel at the superb flora and fauna of this region. Lovely, simply lovely. At the southern exit of the park we made an unplanned overnight stay in Cherokee, North Carolina. Early the next morning we stopped at the Oconaluftee Indian Village, an attraction intent on providing visitors with as authentic an experience as possible of eighteenth-century Cherokee village life.

We were the first to arrive that morning, allowing us a personal teaching guide. The experience was a delight in many ways, and it came to my mind this afternoon because of the Cherokee tradition of appointing two men to tend the central fire of the village from which all other fires were lit. It was a position of high honor in Cherokee society but it carried with it the grave consequence of death if the fire was ever allowed to go out.

So, tonight I am tending my fire. Whenever I wake up, I stoke the fire some. My supply of oak wood is limited so I am using a mixture of the fast-burning pine and the longer-burning oak. Anyway, at about three in the morning I awake to find my fire reduced to barely flickering embers. Quickly, I place kindling and a medium-sized log on the embers; my informal rule being not to use matches. I wait . . . and wait a bit longer. Finally a blaze springs up, keeping my reputation as the tender of the fire intact!

This little story has no essential connection to humility . . . I just wanted to write out the experience. However, an unintended connection to humility did occur. After reviving my fire I pick up my iPad and key in John Michael Talbot's worship album *Come to the Quiet*. With this meditative music by my side I slip back into sleep only to be startled awake several minutes later by the words from the song,

> My sacrifice is a contrite spirit;
> a humble heart you will not spurn.

That was all, and with these words I fall into a restful sleep.

Lenten Meditation 4—Naming and Subsequent Renaming

Sites that are sacred to the Lakota people abound in the Black Hills. For centuries they have been used for vision quests, burials, and other religious ceremonies. One such site is Black Elk Peak (formerly Harney Peak), the tallest point in the Black Hills. The naming and subsequent renaming of this mountain is significant.

The ancient Lakota people referred to this mountain as *Hinhán Káǧa* or "Owl Maker," after the owl-looking rock formations along its ridge. In 1855 it was named Harney Peak to honor the US General William S. Harney who gained fame for his military campaigns against the Lakota people following the Custer massacre at Little Bighorn.

Harney's successes were also his undoing. In 1855 Harney was the commander of a military campaign known today as the Battle of Blue Water Creek, which resulted in the wholesale massacre of Lakota women and children. For fifty years Lakota leaders had tried to have the name of the peak changed. A key figure in these efforts was Basil Brave Heart (of the Pine Ridge Reservation and a Korean War veteran) who argued that General Harney had disgraced the military by his actions. Finally, on August 11, 2016, the mountain's name was changed from "Harney Peak" to "Black Elk Peak." The spokesman for the federal US Board on Geographic Names said of their decision, "In this case, the board felt that the name [Harney Peak] was derogatory or offensive, being that it was on a holy site of Native Americans."

Black Elk was an early twentieth-century Lakota religious leader best known to us for his 1932 book *Black Elk Speaks*, which I read back in 1981 and was moved by it endlessly. At the age of nine Black Elk received his "Great Vision" atop this very mountain. He writes,

> I was standing on the highest mountain of them all, and round about beneath me was the whole hoop of the world. And while I stood there I saw more than I can tell and I understood more than I saw: for I was seeing in a sacred manner the shapes of all things in the spirit, and the shape of all shapes as they must live together like one being.

I bow in Lenten repentance at the arrogance of naming a central sacred site of the Black Hills after such a ruthless military figure. And I bow in humble thanksgiving that *Hinhán Káǧa* is now associated with a name of honor, Black Elk.

PART II

The Moons of Renewal and Growth

(SPRING—*WETÚ*)

The Moon When the Ducks Come Back

MARCH 26–APRIL 22

*Humble yourselves therefore under the mighty hand
of God, so that he may exalt you in due time.*

1 PETER 5:6

*The truly gospel-humble person is not a self-hating person
or a self-loving person, but a self-forgetful person.*

TIMOTHY KELLER

(((((FIRST WEEK)))))

RESPECT TOWARD ALL BEINGS

The third Lakota virtue is *Wawoohola*, "respect." I especially appreciate the teaching about this virtue: "A basic teaching among all tribes was that of respect towards all beings (sentient and insentient) which includes plants, animals, stones, wind, little people, and all of creation. . . . Our Lakota ancestors would ceremonially hunt their bison which would provide clothing, shelter and food for the people. Every part was used and their spirit was honored by placing their skull facing east to meet the rising sun in unison with the rhythm of life."

How important this virtue is in our day of rampant intolerance. Respect for all who are marginalized, "the sat upon, spat upon, ratted on." Respect even for insentient or inanimate creation. This calls us to a deeply sensitive creation care. This description says it beautifully: "plants, animals, stones, wind, little people, and all of creation."

I Too Rejoice

The title for this month draws me in, "The Moon When the Ducks Come Back." I am intrigued by this focus on ducks. My experience is with the mallard duck though I know there are many other varieties. The mallard male with its iridescent green head, bright yellow bill, and black tail curl is both distinctive and quite beautiful. I enjoy the female too though her mottled brown features keep her more in the background. It makes me smile to observe a mother mallard leading her young of seven or eight through a reedy pond. So, I too rejoice when the ducks come back.

The Contrast Is Humbling

Today I walk through a Veterans Memorial Cemetery, which I have passed by numerous times before without ever setting foot inside. It seems like an odd decision for me to turn into a cemetery dedicated to military veterans. I know no one buried here and, besides, my theological convictions incline me toward pacifism.

The decision to turn into the cemetery is simple really. I do not feel up for a hike in the canyon today and I am looking for an alternative that would give me a good walk in the sun before the snowstorm that is predicted for tomorrow arrives.

It is a moving, even humbling, experience to walk among the graves of so many who have served throughout our history, from the Civil War to the present. Yes, I discovered nine graves of Civil War veterans. This surprised me somewhat. Here in Colorado we are far removed from the great sites of the Civil War: Bull Run and Shiloh and Antietam and Vicksburg and Chancellorsville and Gettysburg and more. Plus, judging by eastern standards this is a comparatively new cemetery, being established in 1883 as I remember.

These Civil War graves particularly piqued my interest as I am right now watching the majestic Ken Burns nine-part documentary on the Civil War. Viewing these films for the past month or so I have been repeatedly struck by the contrast between this massive conflagration and my simple task, alone in my study writing on humility. One might say that the contrast is humbling.

My Desires Are Bent

The church liturgy confesses our "disordered affections." But this way of expressing it is far too mild, far too respectable for my condition. My affections, my desires are bent . . . warped . . . twisted . . . turned in on myself.

O Lord, please, I ask, straighten out my affections. Turn my desires in a life-giving, Godward direction. Please. Thank you. Amen.

Leaping for Joy

Well, I was wrong when I said the other week that I was having the final fire of the season. Today we have a "cyclone blizzard" upon us . . . so says the meteorologist. Not because of the amount of snow . . . we'll only get a foot or so. No, it's the snow combined with the high winds that are blowing the snow horizontally and in wild swirls causing near white-out conditions that makes it a cyclone blizzard. I can see our flocked trees only out about fifty feet. All the schools and most businesses are closed for the day, and the major freeway arteries are now shutting down. Carolynn and I have decided to stay tucked in. A perfect day for another fire!

Something about the fire quiets me. A strong cup of coffee and a crackling fire and I am set. I don't really read and I don't really pray . . . at least not in any normal sense. The flames cause a simple meditative mode of sorts. Still. Quiet. Watching the flames swirling up and around kindling and sticks and logs—at times roaring and then a steady burn and in time subsiding to glowing coals. I must say that the logs blazing away is far more entertaining and interesting than television. Plus, the fire has none of those pesky commercials.

Oh, one more thing: if the electricity does go out, the fireplace is our sole source of heat. So, I'll keep the fire burning—crackling and popping and leaping for joy.

(((((SECOND WEEK)))))

AN ACCURATE ASSESSMENT

I really hate to take issue with one of the great saints of the church, Bernard of Clairvaux. It is his well-known definition of humility that rankles me a bit. He wrote, "Humility is a virtue by which a man has a low opinion of himself because he knows himself well." The phrase "a low opinion of himself" is what is hard for me to swallow. No doubt I am reacting to the long history of "worm theology" that has done so much damage in our day. And, of course, the modern psychological concern for a healthy self-esteem is an important factor also.

Likely I am not so much taking issue with the good doctor as I am attempting to translate him into our contemporary context. If I can reinterpret just a bit, I think Bernard is trying to get at the importance of our being able to enter into an accurate assessment of who we really are. This is the point of his underscoring the need for us to know ourselves well. I appreciate this phrase. And knowing ourselves well does indeed bring us down close to the earth, *humus*.

Of course, it is quite arrogant of me to think I can correct one of the most profound Christian thinkers ever. I'll leave it at that.

LENTEN MEDITATION 5—MY HEART IS SADDENED

In the twentieth century the Lakota Nation began a concerted legal effort to reclaim the Black Hills. One federal judge who reviewed the case in the 1970s noted, "A more ripe and rank case of dishonorable dealing will never, in all probability, be found in our history." After a century of legal battles the US Supreme Court in a landmark 1980 decision recognized the eight Lakota Nations' right to the Black Hills as specified in the 1868 treaty. However, rather than ordering the government to return the land, the Lakotas were awarded $105 million for the Black Hills. Despite being among the poorest reservations in the country the Lakotas rejected the payment . . . they wanted their land back. Also, they refused to accept the money on the grounds that one cannot buy and sell sacred land. Johnson Holy Rock, a Lakota elder, writes, "We don't think of the air and water in terms of dollars and cents." And Rick Two-Dogs, a Lakota religious leader, explains, "All of our origin stories go back to this place. We have a spiritual connection to the Black Hills that can't be sold. I don't think I could face the Creator with an open heart if I ever took money for it." Today the Lakotas are found mostly in five reservations: Rosebud Indian Reservation, Pine Ridge Indian Reservation, Lower Brulé Indian Reservation, Cheyenne River Indian Reservation, and Standing Rock Indian Reservation.

In the midst of all this tangled history my heart is saddened for the unjust seizure of the Black Hills from the Lakota people. I wish I could dream up ways to rectify the wrongs done. I cannot. I simply stand and weep inwardly.

A Wide Influence

Now is a good time for me to interact with two significant pieces of writing on humility that have had a wide influence over the centuries. It is important to work on them together, as one builds on the other. The two pieces I am talking about are *The Rule* by Benedict of Nursia (sixth century) and *The Steps of Humility and Pride* by Bernard of Clairvaux (tenth century).

Benedict wrote his rule to bring order and stability to a special problem of that day of roving prophets who had no oversight, no accountability, no stability. I think it would be accurate to say that Benedict's work and the movement that grew out of it has led to monasticism as we know it today. But it was not easy: the first group Benedict gathered under his leadership attempted to poison him!

The heart of *The Rule* is chapter seven, which describes Benedict's "Twelve Steps of Humility," which were to provide a kind of loving structure to the community life of the monastery.

Bernard of Clairvaux was the key leader of a renewal effort within the Benedictine movement, which eventually led to the founding of the Cistercians, a kind of contemplative branch of the Benedictine order. Bernard is best known for his writings on love, especially *On Loving God*. But his first piece of writing was a commentary of sorts on Benedict's "Twelve Steps of Humility." Bernard didn't, however, just stick with the subject of humility. Oh, no. He also took up the opposite inclination, what he called, "The Descending Steps of Pride." In time this writing has become known as *The Steps of Humility and Pride*. In the next few weeks I'll see if I can gain some insights into humility and pride from these two works.

A Truly Helpful Metaphor

In laying out his thoughts on humility Benedict begins by setting before us a truly helpful metaphor (although I find his exegesis of the text rather suspect). Benedict uses the story of Jacob's dream of a ladder with angels ascending and descending and applies it to humility and pride. Here is how he puts it:

> If we want to reach the highest summit of humility . . . then by our ascending actions we must set up that ladder on which Jacob in a dream saw *angels descending and ascending (Gen 28:12)*. Without doubt, this descent and ascent can signify only that we descend by exaltation and ascend by humility. Now the ladder erected is our life on earth, and if we humble our hearts the Lord will raise it to heaven. We may call our body and soul the sides of this ladder, into which our divine vocation has fitted the various steps of humility and discipline as we ascend.

I am well acquainted with the story of Jacob's ladder. The image has been drilled into my subconscious both from Sunday school teachings on Genesis 28 and from singing the spiritual "We Are Climbing Jacob's Ladder," which grew out of the African American slave experience.

The metaphor of a ladder to ascend in our seeking after humility is helpful. Although, since in Jacob's dream angels were both ascending and descending, the metaphor of descent might fit the idea of humility better. I know, I know, Benedict is using the ascending metaphor in order to capture the image of movement upward to heaven. Still . . .

I'm Intrigued by the First Step

Benedict's first two steps up into humility apply easily to all persons. The first step is for us to keep the fear of God always before our eyes and never forget it (Ps 35:2). The second step is for us to love not our own will nor take pleasure in the satisfaction of personal desires; rather we are to imitate by our actions that saying of the Lord: "I have come . . . not to do my own will, but the will of him who sent me" (Jn 6:38).

Beginning with the third step the instructions become specific to the monk entering the monastery. Hence, these steps deal with issues like obedience to the abbot and ways of living in loving submission to one another in the community. To apply these steps to the common person today demands considerable reinterpretation . . . and this is exactly what those who teach Benedictine spirituality do when speaking to the general populace.

But I'm intrigued by the first step into humility (to keep the fear of God always before our eyes and never forget it). What immediately caught my attention is the fact that Benedict expands on this step more than any of the others. Frankly, it's straightforward enough, not really needing any explanation. Yet Benedict devotes the lion's share of his attention to it. Why? I'm not sure, I'm just wondering. I'll sleep on it.

(((((THIRD WEEK)))))

SERVILE FEAR AND *FILIAL* FEAR

The phrasing of Benedict's first step does not sit well with us today. We don't like the language of "the fear of the Lord." For us it brings to mind images of groveling and unthinking obedience. Just to be clear, I don't like the phrase. It feels far too negative.

However, Benedict is merely drawing the phrase from the Bible. Just think of Proverbs 9:10,

> The fear of the LORD is the beginning of wisdom,
>   and the knowledge of the Holy One is insight.

I'm actually helped here by the distinction Martin Luther made between what he called a "*servile* fear" and a "*filial* fear." *Servile* describes fear of being punished for doing something wrong. *Filial* refers to fear of doing something wrong to, or dishonoring of, a loved one. So, the focus of our "fear" needs to be one of awe and reverence for the greatness and the goodness of God. This is a focus severely lacking in contemporary Christianity. Because God invites us into the personal intimacy of Abba, Father, we can easily corrupt the relationship into something flippant and cavalier. Always, always we are to maintain a healthy reverence and adoration of the One who is Creator and Sustainer of all things. Perhaps this is a good reason to retain the language of "the fear of the Lord."

Upward Steps and Downward Steps

By writing on both the upward steps of humility and the downward steps of pride Bernard gives us a helpful insight. The upward steps of humility begin with love of God and in the end result in love of our neighbor. In contrast, the downward steps of pride begin with contempt for our neighbor and in the end result in contempt for God.

How does this help me? Well, if I am beginning to feel contempt for my neighbor, say through gossip, then I need to beware that the seeds of pride are being planted in my heart, and that this will eventually lead me to contempt for God. If I want to learn how to love my neighbor, I begin by learning to love God, and in God's time and in God's way, this will lead me to love my neighbor.

Beautiful Teaching in Humility

Today is Palm Sunday, which leads us into Holy Week and Resurrection Sunday. Palm Sunday is itself a beautiful teaching in humility. We are all accustomed to children waving palm branches in church services to remind us of Jesus riding into Jerusalem on a donkey and the people waving palm branches and shouting, "Hosanna! Blessed is the one who comes in the name of the Lord— the King of Israel!" (Jn 12:13). In Bibles and in church bulletins this is described as "Jesus' Triumphal Entry into Jerusalem." We tend to forget that this scene is in direct contrast to the Roman triumphal entries replete with trumpets and generals on mighty steeds and parades of marching troops. For a modern analogy we might want to think of today's military parades of tanks and surface-to-air missiles and marching troops.

Jesus' entry into Jerusalem is the exact opposite of these egocentric displays of might and power and domination. No, Jesus' entry was on a donkey with a spontaneous display of the people's love and affection for this "man of sorrows." Not a hint here of the intimidation and oppression so blatant in the kings and emperors of the first century . . . and of our day. This is the humility of Jesus as king . . . a king who would "not break a bruised reed or quench a smoldering wick" (Mt 12:20; Is 42:3). King Jesus, you see, will never crush the needy nor snuff out the smallest hope.

MY HEART BOWS

In the Christian calendar today is called "Maundy Thursday." The name is derived from the Latin *mandatum,* meaning "command" . . . think of the contemporary word *mandate.* This naming comes from the extended teaching that Jesus gives between two monumental events. Theologians call this teaching "the upper room discourse," and right at the heart of this teaching Jesus says, "I give you a new commandment, that you love one another. Just as I have loved you, you also should love one another. By this everyone will know that you are my disciples, if you have love for one another" (Jn 13:34-35). This is the "maundy," the command for us to love one another. So simple. So profound. So life altering as we learn to live into the command.

The two monumental events that bracket this teaching are Jesus' washing of the disciples' feet and his establishing the Lord's Supper, often called the Eucharist. Both events instruct us in Christian humility.

The disciples had gathered in the upper room for the Passover celebration. Their feet were dry, dusty, cracked. The customary servant who would care for this simple, physical need was absent. So, Jesus steps in and washes their feet. Returning to his seat he says, "Do you know what I have done to you? You call me Teacher and Lord—and you are right, for that is what I am. So if I, your Lord and Teacher, have washed your feet, you also ought to wash one another's feet. For I have set you an example that you also should do as I have done to you" (Jn 13:12-15). Wow! A walking example of stark humility. I am humbled simply by reading the words on the page.

The second event is the Passover feast that Jesus and the Twelve celebrate in the upper room. But now Jesus invests this holy rite with a whole new significance. Ever since the great exodus the Passover was celebrated in memory of the death angel "passing over" the children of Israel when they were bound in Egyptian slavery. But on this night Jesus takes the unleavened bread and after giving thanks he breaks it declaring, "this is my body, that is broken for you. Do this in remembrance of me." He next takes the cup of wine declaring, "This cup is the new covenant in my blood. Do this, as often as you drink it, in remembrance of me. For as often as you eat this bread and drink the cup, you proclaim the Lord's death until he comes" (1 Cor 11:23-26). My heart bows in thanksgiving and gratitude!

THE GREAT SACRIFICE

On this Friday followers of "the Way" remember the Great Sacrifice, Jesus' death on the cross. It must stand as the supreme act of humility in all human history.

Jesus' last words on the cross is the triumphal cry, "It is finished!" This was not simply a declaration that his life was ending. Oh, no. Jesus was announcing to all who had ears to hear that this great work of redemption was finished. Jesus on the cross took into himself all of the sin and rebellion of dark humanity and redeemed it by his blood. All the sorrows throughout all time. All the cries. All the sufferings. All the barbarous cruelty. All the screams. All of it . . . he took it into himself and redeemed it. Hence, the triumphant word, "It is finished."

It humbles me, this great act of redemption. Words fail me. All I can do is kneel in silent worship and adoration at the foot of the cross.

A MINORITY REPORT

I do want to take strong exception to one matter that both Benedict and Bernard refer to . . . namely the issue of humor. From the language that is used I think we can safely assume that both disapprove of it . . . strongly so. Benedict says, "The tenth step of humility is that he is not given to ready laughter." And Bernard in his descending steps of pride comments on the danger of laughter: "At times he simply cannot stop laughing or hide his empty-headed merriment. He is like a well-filled bladder that has been pricked and squeezed. The air, not finding a free vent, whistles out through the little hole with squeak after squeak."

I know, I know, humor can be overdone. Indeed, in certain forms it can be used as a weapon to attack, demean, or destroy. And perhaps both Benedict and Bernard are merely dealing with the ways humor can become a distraction to a focused life with God.

However, I'd like to submit a minority report on behalf of good-hearted laughter. Humor, offered in love, can help build community life. Frankly, an occupational hazard of religious folk is to become stuffy bores. And humor helps to undercut this danger by stoutly refusing to allow us to take ourselves too seriously. It is a grace when we can laugh at our gaffes and foibles. Humor helps us welcome the unexpected and the unpredictable, to relish the ridiculous and the absurd. We don't need to create a huge chasm between prayer and playfulness.

I rather like the observation of Thomas Kelly when, poking a bit of fun at his own tradition, he wrote, "I'd rather be jolly Saint Francis hymning his canticle to the sun than a dour old sobersides Quaker whose diet would appear to have been spiritual persimmons." Well, enough said!

I CAN BUT TEACH WHAT I HAVE LEARNED

Bernard had written his book to one "brother Godfrey" who had asked Bernard to put in writing and expand his sermons "On the Degrees of Humility." Bernard was hesitant to undertake the project because as he put it, "I had my doubts about my own ability." He finally relented and wrote the book, adding, "Should there be anything helpful in what I write, I beg you to pray that I shall not fall victim to pride; or if (as is more likely) I fail to produce anything that is helpful, there will still be no reason for pride."

Bernard, of course, did not confine himself to writing just about humility but added some very helpful material on pride, which is why we now title his writing *The Steps of Humility and Pride*.

Bernard's concluding comment is one of my favorite passages in the entire book. And after I had chided him about his negative view of laughter, I do find this to be high humor . . . of a tenth-century variety. Bernard writes,

> Well, you may perhaps say, brother Godfrey, that in describing the steps of pride instead of the steps of humility, I seem to have gone beyond your request and on to my own course. I can only say that I can but teach what I have learned. I did not think it appropriate for me to speak about the ascent, as I am aware that my own movements tend to be down rather than up. St. Benedict may lay before you the steps of humility, for he held them in his own heart. I have nothing to lay before you, apart from my own downward course. However, if that is examined carefully, you will hopefully discover the way to go up.

NUMEROUS QUESTIONS

Today, Luke 9:46-48 grabs my attention: "An argument arose among them as to which one of them was the greatest. But Jesus, aware of their inner thoughts, took a little child and put it by his side, and said to them, 'Whoever welcomes this child in my name welcomes me, and whoever welcomes me welcomes the one who sent me; for the least among all of you is the greatest.'" This passage raises numerous questions in my mind:

- What caused this argument about who is the greatest to erupt in the first place?
- Why did Jesus use a child to illustrate his teaching about greatness?
- How on a practical level is it that the "the least is the greatest"?

I will try to live into these questions for a while and see what I can learn.

WHO IS THE LEAST?

Whenever human beings are having an argument over who is the greatest, underneath there is a fearful concern over who is the least. Most of us realize that we are not the "greatest" . . . just don't let us be the "least." Perhaps this is why Jesus uses a child to illustrate his point. In that day the child *is* the very least. I rather think things have not changed all that much. When people gather for conversation children are often left out. Or, if the child is allowed into the circle of conversation, it is only to listen and not to speak.

THIS WELCOMING SPIRIT

The child is an appropriate example of "greatness" because of the child's ability to welcome anyone and everyone. It doesn't matter who they are. In the sandbox children may not even know each other, but in a few moments they are happily playing together. Perhaps this welcoming spirit is at the heart of greatness.

A GIGANTIC BOUQUET

Oh my! This morning Castlewood Canyon is completely covered in a gigantic bouquet of wildflowers.

- The delicate lavender *pasque flower* abounds. It is one of the first flowers to emerge and is sometimes called the Easter flower referring to its Easter flowering period. The poet Badger Clark wrote of it as "that bold bit of life at the edge of the snows."
- The pure white petals of the *crownleaf evening primrose* sparkle in the dawn, and its bright yellow stamens wave in the cool morning breeze.
- The charming bud-like pink *prairie smoke flower* is scattered throughout the canyon giving it a special elegance.
- The bright *purple locoweed* spreads itself all along the canyon floor providing a royal welcome trail for the hiker.

I am wondering, *Can flowers be humble?* I don't know, I'm just wondering.

They are certainly not "humble" in the same way as we who struggle with raging pride and destructive self-deception. No, but isn't it true that flowers do reflect something of the character of their Creator? So, I am wondering, *Is the great humility that is in God in some way reflected back in these wonderful wildflowers?* I watch as they show forth such brilliance and beauty without any strutting or puffing whatever. They are simply there for all to see . . . more beautiful than human words can tell. In all the glory of these flowers I am taught a bit about the beauty of humility.

The Moon of Making Fat

APRIL 23–MAY 20

Wisdom is with the humble.

PROVERBS 11:2

One day Anthony of the desert stepped out of his hermitage where he saw all the snares of the devil spread out like a net over the world. He let out a great groan of terror and cried out: "My God! How can anyone be saved?" A voice responded from heaven: "Humility."

ANTHONY OF THE DESERT

(((((FIRST WEEK)))))

STRENGTH OF CHARACTER

The fourth Lakota virtue is *Wayuonihan*, "honor," and it is described like this: "Being honorable means having strength of character by being a good person. Honor goes hand and hand with respect and many of the other virtues. To live the virtues it shows that someone has the integrity and dignity that makes up honor. Humility waters the roots of the tree of honor which then bears the fruit of love. By having honor means that one would choose the path of nonviolence and compassion rather than dishonorable actions."

I am especially glad to see an emphasis on how the virtues interrelate with one another.

Difficulty Understanding

I had difficulty understanding the naming of this particular month. The various efforts to translate *Wihahata Cepapi* into English were confusing. I found everything from "The Moon of Fattening" to "The Moon of Cracking Bones for Marrow Fat." I rather imagine each rendering has something to it in Lakota culture. Then I read one elder's explanation, which, at last, made sense to me. He writes, "This moon is named for the female animals. During this time, those carrying babies were at their largest before giving birth." The Moon of Making Fat. Of course.

A Common Misconception

As I talk with people about the topic of humility and read about it and seek to practice it, I find a common misconception. It is this notion that if I am truly humble, I won't know that I am humble. That is, self-knowledge of humility actually proves that we lack it. And I see people getting themselves all tied up in knots about this, and end up having to lie to themselves, saying that they couldn't possibly have humility when they do indeed possess this finest of virtues.

The end result of this misconception is to cause people to forsake any effort toward humility. And then they are completely baffled about how to understand the many passages from Scripture that urge them to seek out humility. "Have unity of spirit, sympathy, love for one another, a tender heart, and a *humble* mind" (1 Pet 3:8). "*Humble* yourselves therefore under the mighty hand of God" (1 Pet 5:6). "All who *humble* themselves will be exalted" (Lk 18:14). "As God's chosen ones, holy and beloved, clothe yourselves with compassion, kindness, *humility*, meekness, and patience" (Col 3:12). "Whoever becomes *humble* like this child is the greatest in the kingdom of heaven" (Mt 18:4). And on and on.

Is there anything that can be done to correct this misconception? Yes, indeed. One simple place to begin is by paying attention to the antithesis of humility—pride—that we see in others. We observe all the strutting and puffing and efforts to be the center of attention. We observe these things without any judgment or condemnation whatsoever. Indeed, this process likely helps to reveal hidden corners in our own lives where we too are strutting and puffing and wanting to be the center of all things.

Next, it helps us to observe a healthy humility functioning in others. These things are not hard to see if we will simply watch and listen. We see the quiet confidence a person has around others, the easy laughter, the almost reflexive lifting up of others in the group.

Now, we do not attempt to imitate this behavior—this would only lead us to a destructive outward legalism. No, we simply observe its good effects on everyone concerned, and then we hold this picture firmly in our mind.

Finally, in seeking after humility it is of utmost importance that we follow the principle of indirection. We do not try to attain humility directly. Oh, no . . . that will only serve to inflame our pride. No, we come at the matter indirectly. We simply take up those things that, in God's time and in God's way, will lead us into the virtue of humility. An obvious example is the spiritual discipline of service. We discover multiplied ways of serving others. And as we do these things something solid begins to be built deep within us.

I don't know how this works exactly. Well, of course, I don't know. This is the work of divine grace and we humans can never fully understand the hidden workings of grace. God, it seems, is taking these simple acts and somehow using them to turn us and turn us and turn us until "we come round right," as the old Shaker hymn puts it. All of this is interior work in the deep recesses of the heart. But it does have outward effects. We begin by noticing people we had never noticed before. We start to care about people in newer, deeper ways. We find genuine joy in the success of others. In some measure we are enabled to enter the pain and sorrow of others. Things like that.

As this process goes forward we begin to detect the growth of humility deep within ourselves. Now, here is the beauty in all this: we feel no need to make anything of this change. The old strutting and puffing and seeking for attention simply does not drive us like it used to . . . or even appeal to us.

Now, these results are far beyond our ability to produce. God alone can change the inner workings of the heart. Indeed, this is one way we can know that what is happening is an action of divine grace. And so, we simply give thanks to God for the growth of humility that is coming into our hearts.

THE DESTRUCTIVE CHARACTER OF HUMILIATION

I am wanting to clarify in my mind the distinction between the virtue of humility and the issue of humiliation that is so prevalent in our culture.

Humility as a virtue is a grace that is given by God. We participate with God in this grace-filled work by taking up disciplines appropriate for the development of humility. Service is the discipline that is supreme in this effort. Solitude also seems important . . . and silence too. At any rate, we take up activities that will draw us close to the earth—*humus*—and help us develop deep in our soul a right relationship with others and with God.

There is also the action of humbling ourselves. In my mind this appears to be a freely chosen action of recognizing God's wonderful, loving, care-filled authority over us.

Humiliation, on the other hand, is an action by others and is done to demean or destroy the individual. School children mock and laugh at an autistic child. A boss demeans the work of a laborer. A parent ridicules a child. Humiliation always seeks to dishonor, to discredit, to tear down. I wonder if those who participate in such actions have deep-seated fears about their own adequacy.

So, we seek after true humility of spirit and never to seek the humiliation of another human being.

PRIDE TOPPLED BY HUMILITY

Today I find myself meditating on the enormous contribution of Evagrius of Pontus (fourth century) to our understanding of the moral life. He constructed for us "the eight godly virtues" which we are to use to destroy what he called "the eight deadly thoughts."

These insights grew out of a near catastrophic moral failure for Evagrius himself. Evagrius was a rising star in Constantinople, a legend in his own time. He was well positioned for high ecclesiastical office. But then, right in the midst of ministry work, he fell madly in love with a married woman. Sabotaged by his own passions, and fearful of them, Evagrius fled to the Egyptian desert, never to return to Constantinople.

Here in the desert Evagrius first hammers out the "eight deadly thoughts," vices that destroy our lives . . . gluttony and anger and greed and envy and pride and lust and sloth and melancholy. But he does not stop here. He next proceeds to set before us the "eight godly virtues" through which we are, under God, to overcome the deadly thoughts. In Evagrius's thinking we develop the virtue of temperance in order to conquer gluttony; the virtue of mildness allows us to conquer anger; the virtue of generosity to conquer greed; the virtue of happiness to conquer envy; the virtue of humility to conquer pride; the virtue of chastity to conquer lust; the virtue of diligence to conquer sloth, and the virtue of wisdom to conquer melancholy.

My interest in this list is to understand exactly how it is that *humility* conquers *pride*. In ordinary human life pride seems to be so strong; humility appears so weak. Exactly how is it that humility can overcome pride? Pride—this inordinate belief in our own importance—how can it be toppled by something like humility, which by all appearances seems so fragile, so delicate, so feeble? I will spend the next days to see if I can gain some light on this matter.

(((((SECOND WEEK)))))

This Contrast of Humility and Pride

It is interesting to see how this contrast of humility and pride runs through all the moral-formation literature. I just discussed the thoughts of Evagrius in the fourth century. Here is a helpful statement of C. S. Lewis in the twentieth century, "There is one vice of which no man in the world is free; which every one in the world loathes when he sees it in someone else; and of which hardly any people . . . ever imagine that they are guilty themselves. . . . The vice I am talking of is Pride or Self-Conceit: and the virtue opposite to it, in Christian morals, is called Humility."

The Child in Need of Christ's Mothering Love

I think it would be helpful to gain a woman's perspective on humility. The first woman that comes to my mind and the very best person that I can think of is Julian of Norwich and her *Revelations of Divine Love*. Julian is the first woman to write in the English language . . . well, Middle English to be exact. I have found an essay by Grace Hamman that is a rich resource for my study.

Julian is well-known for the extended metaphor she gives of God and Christ as a Mother and the believer as her child. She writes,

As truly as God is our Father, so truly is God our Mother, and he revealed that in everything, and especially in these sweet words where he says: "I am he; that is to say: I am he, the power and goodness of fatherhood; I am he, the wisdom and the lovingness of motherhood; I am he, the light and the grace which is all blessed love, I am he, the Trinity; I am he, the unity; I am he, the great supreme goodness of every kind of thing. . . ." As truly is God our Father, so truly is God our Mother. Our Father wills, our Mother works, our good Lord the Holy Spirit confirms.

In chapter sixty Julian speaks of "our true Mother Jesus" and "our precious Mother Jesus" and "our tender Mother Jesus."

In the literature on Julian much has been made of the "Mother" metaphor for Christ; however, precious little attention has been given to the metaphor of us as the child. Julian's emphasis on us as the child in need of Christ's mothering love is creative and genuinely helpful. Julian gives special attention to the virtue of humility and meekness. The *Middle English Dictionary* defines *meek* and *humble* as essentially synonymous terms. Meekness appears in some form about fifty-eight times in Julian's *Revelation of Divine Love*. It is developed in the child, especially as we learn of our own sinfulness and distance from God. She explores the "intimate dependence" of the child.

Most medieval contemplative writers depict virtue formation as a hierarchy of knowledge developed by ladders, scales, or steps—think of John Climacus's *The Ladder of Divine Ascent* or Walter Hilton's *Scale of Perfection*. In contrast, Julian's imagery of the mother and child explores a process of growth more like the demanding days involved in raising a child. No straightforward ladder of progress here. No, Julian sees a long process of daily development. Hamman writes, "Julian's similitude of the mother and child explores a process of change much like the repetitive days of child-raising, . . . the long process and ever repeating forms of the day-to-day tending to a child's physical, moral, and, most notably, spiritual formation."

Another difference with Julian: while emphasizing the importance of us recognizing "that we have sinned grievously in this life" there is no responding condemnation from God. Julian writes, "The sweet gracious hands of our Mother are ready and diligent about us; for he in all this work exercises the true office of a kind nurse, who has nothing else to do but attend to the safety of her child."

Most certainly there is a learning and a growing in all this. Julian writes, "the humility and meekness which we shall obtain by the sight of our fall, for by that we shall be raised high in heaven, to which raising we might never have come without that meekness."

Well, there is certainly a learning and a growing for me in all this. I'll need to live with Julian's writings for a while. Julian both tantalizes me and frustrates me.

(((((THIRD WEEK)))))

DESIRE GONE AWRY

I rather think that pride seems so strong because it orients all our desires and all our appetites around the *self*. The human self becomes the most central thing in our thinking and our living. Add to this that a key element in pride is the love of power. It contains this need to control and manage everything . . . and everybody. Then, third, note the close connection between pride and narcissism. Hence, pride is the ultimate example of desire gone awry. These factors exert an enormous pull on the self, making pride seem very strong indeed.

A Centripetal Force

On the other hand, humility contains a tremendous centripetal force to pull us inward toward the center, into the way we are meant to live. It continually draws us into what is natural, what is authentic, what is real. Pride is always a distortion of who we are truly created to be.

Humility is so very appealing when we see it in another person. Conversely, when we watch someone consumed with pride it feels unnatural, deformed, twisted. Humility is beautiful, whereas pride is ugly.

Our Longing for Worth and Dignity

Humility affirms our longing for worth and dignity. It teaches us how much God delights in us, how much we matter to God, how significant we are to God, even how honorable we are to God. It rightly orders our search for worth and dignity.

Pride does exactly the opposite. It perverts these desires and turns them in on themselves. When the vice of pride reigns supreme we *must* be the center of everything. We *must* have. We *must* possess. We *must* win.

Humility Is Divine Gift

We do not come by humility on our own. It is God who initiates contact with us, and not our own activity that leads us to God. We cannot manufacture God's initiative. Ultimately humility is a gift from God. However, we can prepare for the grace of humility by orienting our will toward God.

If I am right in saying that humility is divine gift, then we can be assured that it is strong indeed. Strong enough even to break the bonds of pride.

(((((FOURTH WEEK)))))

Exactly How It Is That Humility Conquers Pride

The other day I was visiting with Pat, an especially gifted spiritual director. I asked her to reflect with me on exactly how it is that humility conquers pride. In the midst of the visit Pat mentioned a recent experience from one of the persons she meets with and felt this might cast some light on the issue I was grappling with. I invited her to write the experience out in an email, being sure to protect the individual's confidentiality. Here is what Pat wrote:

"Katie" (not real name) was the leader of a ministry retreat event. She had a leadership team functioning with her. Different talk topics were assigned to leadership team members and one member of the leadership insisted that she do a certain talk because that is what she knew best and could do best. Katie also wanted to do this talk and she did not know how well this other woman would do (pride). Now Katie is someone who likes to make everyone happy so it would have been the "normal" thing for her to give into the other person's wants but then carry resentment toward that person (also pride). Instead, she spent time contemplating what was going on within (space to allow God's work within). As Katie prayed she realized that she really did not HAVE to do that talk. She could take it or leave it (detachment). Katie then chose to give the talk to the other lady (choice) not out of wanting that other woman to think she was a good leader or like her but out of a free choice. Katie told me how the other woman did very well; Katie was happy for her. Best of all, Katie said that she experienced new freedom (humility) and rejoiced in a bit of transformation in her life.

This is exactly what I am after. It goes directly to the heart attitude and not just superficial actions. It describes well how pride works in a specific relationship situation and how it can be overcome in the spirit of humility. May I be more like "Katie"!

A Wonderful Freedom from Self-Absorption

Today I sit and watch people going about their daily tasks. I listen to the conversations that go on. I notice their body language.

Some, it seems, are working hard to impress others. Some appear timid and fearful. Some are loud and appear determined to dominate everyone else. Still others seem to be adjusting their position relative to the group.

But a distinct few seem quite different. They listen to others with genuine interest. They speak easily but not to impress, only to participate in the conversation. They have an unusual ease about themselves. Most of all they are marked by a wonderful freedom from self-absorption. These, I think, are the truly humble ones.

The Moon of the Green Leaves

MAY 21–JUNE 17

Walk side by side in harmony with each other.
Try to feel what others feel. Love each other as family.
Be tenderhearted and walk with a humble spirit.

1 PETER 3:8 FIRST NATIONS VERSION

It does not require many words to speak the truth.

CHIEF JOSEPH OF THE NEZ PERCE

(((((FIRST WEEK)))))

LOVE RULES OVER ALL THINGS

I am glad for the fifth Lakota virtue, *Cantognake*, "love." Here is how this virtue is described: "More than just compassion, love is having the flame of emotion in one's heart. Love rules over all things. The whole universe exists because of love. It is the motive of all creation."

I'm glad for their emphasis on the centrality of love as a virtue we should all seek after.

SUCH MULTIFACETED BEAUTIES

"The Moon of the Green Leaves" . . . oh my, what a lovely understatement. To be sure every tree, every plant is bursting forth with various shades of green. But there is more. The multicolored flowers fill the senses. The warblers and the robins add song to the color. We have two barred owls who have started hooting back and forth to each other in the evenings. Oh, and I can't forget the ruby-throated hummingbird that is building a nest under our deck. So, the Lakota calendar speaks well when it reminds us that this is "The Moon of the Green Leaves."

I am wondering if the virtue of humility is advanced among those who can revel in such multifaceted beauties! I'm not sure, just wondering.

CLOTHE YOURSELVES WITH HUMILITY

This morning I am drawn to the counsel of our friend Peter, older now . . . and wiser. In his first letter he counsels "elders" on how they are to "tend the flock of God" (1 Pet 5:1-5). I'm especially taken by the gentleness in his instructions to those with leadership responsibilities, "Do not lord it over those in your charge, but be examples to the flock." Next, he gives counsel to the younger ones to "accept the authority of the elders." And finally, he gives wise instruction to both groups, "elders" and "younger": "And all of you must clothe yourselves with humility in your dealings with one another, for 'God opposes the proud, but gives grace to the humble.'"

I rather like Eugene Peterson's rendering of this passage in *The Message*:

> But all of you, leaders and followers alike, are to be down to earth with each other, for—
>
> > God has had it with the proud,
> > But takes delight in just plain people.

Eugene's "down to earth with each other" is a helpful way to unpack humility. It brings to mind once again the most basic notion of humility as tied to the earth, *humus*. Of course the metaphor from the New Revised Standard Version (NRSV), "clothe yourselves with humility," is suggestive too. We might think of completely wrapping ourselves up in a cloak of humility so that the only part of us showing is our face. Of course, doing this in practice is the key. At home. At work. In our thoughts. Hum! I'll want to work with this for a while and see what I can learn.

(((((SECOND WEEK)))))

ACHIEVING SUCCESS WITHOUT FORFEITING HUMILITY

Of late I have been scratching my head to think of individuals of prominence who are characterized by humility. Then today in the midst of my musings I received a copy of the new edition of Philip Yancey's two books that he wrote years ago with the surgeon Dr. Paul Brand, now rolled into one and titled *Fearfully and Wonderfully*. In his new preface Philip warmly describes the life and medical career of Dr. Brand.

Twice Philip's description caused me to catch my breath. First, after listing the many accolades Dr. Brand has received over a lifetime of distinguished service, Philip adds, "Despite such international recognition, humility struck me as his strongest attribute." Humility his strongest attribute! Yes, indeed. May this quality of life be seen more and more on the face of the earth.

Philip movingly shares some of his personal struggles with faith early in his writing career—think of *Disappointment with God* and *Where Is God When It Hurts?* Much of Philip's early struggles came from exposure to what he describes as "toxic churches." But here he relates to us a contrasting experience, the transforming experience resulting from a decade and more working with Paul Brand. He writes, "I can imagine God gently steering me to Dr. Brand . . . at a critical time in my spiritual journey. *OK, Philip, you've seen some of the worst the church has to offer. Now I'll show you one of the best.*"

Through his extended relationship with Paul Brand a new assurance crept into Philip's faith, an "assurance that the Christian life I had heard in theory can actually work out in practice. It is indeed possible to live in modern society, achieve success without forfeiting humility, serve others sacrificially, and yet emerge with joy and contentment."

My mind came to a full stop on the phrase "achieve success without forfeiting humility." I gasped. What a vivid example of exactly the combination I had been searching for.

I've known humble people who were not especially successful and successful people who exhibited precious little humility. But the combination of "success without forfeiting humility" . . . this is rare indeed.

And note, Philip did not come to this insight by reading a book but by observing a life. Good for Philip. Good for Paul Brand.

In a personal note Philip wrote to me, "I wish you could have known him!" Me too. Such sterling character formation is rare in our day.

Our Moral Landscape

As I pondered further on this combined quality of "success without forfeiting humility" several other individuals did come to mind. I thought of Rosa Parks and Dag Hammarskjöld and John Glenn. I'm sure there are more fine examples. Still, the rarity of this combination is what strikes me. And it causes me to wonder why our moral landscape appears so barren in this regard. I will think on it.

Those Who Best Bear His Mild Yoke

I've been meditating of late on John Milton's famous sonnet, "When I Consider How My Light Is Spent." Sometimes it is titled "On His Blindness," and Milton is clearly struggling with the personal tragedy of his own coming blindness. And not only his blindness but human tragedies of every sort. He wrestles with these frailties and wonders how we can serve God with such limiting capacities. In reply he learns that "God doth not need / Either man's work or his own gifts." No, it is those "who best / Bear his mild yoke, they serve him best."

To be sure, "Thousands at his bidding speed / And post o'er Land and Ocean without rest." But, and here is the central reality for Milton . . . and for us, "They also serve who only stand and wait."

Milton here is giving us a posture of humility in its most fundamental form. In his approaching blindness Milton "sees" that the act of service given to him is to "stand and wait." Nothing more. Nothing less. This is how he is to bear Christ's "mild yoke." Oh, may I have the same perfect vision.

The Most Damaging Fall for the Soul

I am sipping an Americano coffee at the Owl's Nest, a nearby coffee shop. (Well, it's eight miles away . . . nothing is "nearby" to our home.) I find it a good place to read because it is offers a quiet setting rather than piped in music. Today I come across this observation of Evagrius, "Pride is the cause of the most damaging fall for the soul." I've read this sentence before but today the thought carries greater weight.

It is, of course, easy to see this "fall of the soul" in the vicious despots and horrible dictators that march across the pages of history. However, I should also watch my own life to see if there is anywhere I can detect personally a "damaging fall for the soul."

I remember Evagrius's teaching that humility conquers pride. This is the cure for the "damaging fall for the soul." May it be so for me and may it be so for all who suffer from the ravages of pride.

(((((THIRD WEEK)))))

"My Life Is Hid in Him That Is My Treasure"

Today I am seeking to meditate on George Herbert's poem "Colossians 3:3." Herbert takes the phrase from Colossians "your life is hid with Christ in God" and inserts it diagonally through the poem. Interestingly he personalizes the phrase by changing "your life" to "my life." Inserted diagonally are the words, "My Life Is Hid in Him That Is My Treasure."

What catches me today is his use of the phrase "double motion,"

My words and thoughts do both express this notion,
That **Life** hath with the sun a double motion.

His "double motion" describes how we all live on both a horizontal and a vertical level. Outwardly we are carrying on the tasks of our day: doing laundry, talking with clients, working at our computer. This is the horizontal motion. Yet underneath, deeper down, our life is hid with Christ in God. And it is here in the innermost sanctuary of the soul that the real, substantive work of spiritual formation goes on. This is the vertical motion.

This inward reality remains out of sight to all but the most spiritually sensitive. The outward is always clamoring and demanding. The inward is silent and never draws attention to itself. If we satisfy the outward, we receive acclaim. If we satisfy the inward, we receive nothing. Well, nothing outwardly—inwardly we experience a life of righteousness, peace, and joy in the Holy Spirit.

We must, however, remember that this is a "double" motion. It isn't as if the outward is bad and the inward good. Oh, no! It is that the inward is central and the outward flows out of the inward. As we give attention to that which is central, the outward tasks of life become more like a reflex action to the prior initiation of the heart. A double motion.

I am coming to see humility as among the most silent and unobtrusive of the inward works of the heart. And among the most important.

Nature's Softening Influence

Tonight I find the Lakota concern for creation care helpful. I'm instructed by the words of Chief Luther Standing Bear, "for the Lakota there was no wilderness, because nature was not dangerous but hospitable, not forbidding but friendly. The old Lakota was wise. He knew that man's heart, away from nature, becomes hard; he knew that lack of respect for growing, living things soon led to lack of respect for humans, too. So he kept his children 'close to nature's softening influence.'"

These words are especially instructive because of the connection he makes between character formation and our personal nearness to the earth. Today people argue over the causes of climate change and the ways in which we are to steward the earth. Yet, all these discussions still leave us in charge; how we are to do this and not do that. See, we remain in charge.

Rather, Chief Standing Bear reminds us to bend down near the earth and learn from the earth. This is an act of humility. And it is where we experience "nature's softening influence," as he puts it.

((((FOURTH WEEK)))))

MY INSULATED BUBBLE

I begin this day tied to the computer responding to multiple problematic emails. I stay with it until about 2:00 p.m. At this point I feel my brain fried and so decide to go to the rec center for a small workout. The whole time at the rec center my mind is wrapped up with those pesky emails . . . "Did I said what was needed? How do I respond to the emails still unanswered?" The whole time I am in an insulated bubble completely disregarding those around me. I finish with the weights and return to the locker room still oblivious to all those around me. I shower, dress, and begin to make my way out.

As I am ascending the winding stairs toward the front desk the afternoon sun shines brightly through the large picture window blinding me for the final four or five steps. Once on the landing and regaining my sight I nearly run into a rather large man preparing to make the descent down those same steps. We are only two feet apart. He breaks into a warm, broad smile and stammers out a "hello!" He holds a cane in his right hand and clearly struggles to maneuver his left side. I surmise that he likely has had a stroke and is working on recovery. We greet briefly and I step aside. Being careful not to stare I watch out of the corner of my eye that he is not using the elevator and instead is walking down the stairs one slow step at a time.

Our encounter is a brief one . . . but what a difference it makes. Without trying he has burst my insulated bubble and caused me to become aware of another human being. In addition, I am humbled by his brave determination. I go up and down these stairs with ease . . . howbeit a little more slowly these days. He, on the other hand, must exert great effort just to make it down to the gym floor. I am guessing he has a trainer waiting in the gym to guide him—carefully, painfully—through a series of exercises. In time he may improve. He may not. Nevertheless, he is there determined to take the next step. My anonymous friend teaches me humility.

THE FIRST AND MOST ESSENTIAL ELEMENT

Early this morning I am pondering the strong words of Andrew Murray that humility is "the first and most essential element of discipleship." Wow! When I read these words of Murray I instinctively thought, "of course, he is exactly right." And yet how many years have I viewed other things as "first" and "most essential." *Surely, the first and most essential thing is developing evangelistic skills so as to draw those who are far from God into "the Divine Center." Maybe, memorizing passages of Scripture is first and most essential. Or, perhaps growing in supernatural power in prayer is first and most essential.* On and on.

I simply never would have thought to place humility as "first" and "most essential" in thinking about discipleship. It feels so contrary to modern sensibilities . . . even religious sensibilities. What I failed to understand was pride's corrosive influence in our spirit. It utterly corrupts the heart. And it will destroy our efforts for Christ and his kingdom so subtly, yet so completely. Oh, how we need to experience humility's greater strength to undermine pride and ultimately free us from it.

I now see that in discipleship to Christ we need to train ourselves to fight the devil, defeating the pride-filled arrogance and raging narcissism that plagues modern culture. We need to learn the subtleties of pride that can seep into the innermost chambers of the heart puffing up our ego.

This is the negative side of our training in the way of Christ. More is needed, much more. We need to experience the positive side discovered in humility. Humility is a pristine virtue that first needs to be understood. Second, it needs to be valued. Third, it needs to be faithfully modeled. Fourth, it needs to become a fixed experience in the personality.

Such training demands a loving community. Others are needed to provide us perspective and discernment: a spiritual director, a spiritual friend, perhaps a wise elder. For humility to mature we need a community of persons who know how to lovingly guide another soul. This is what I need most of all.

A BEAUTIFUL HUMILITY

To close out my journal this month I think it will be good if Julian has the last word:

> He [Jesus] says, "Do not blame yourself too much thinking that your trouble and distress is all your fault. For it is not my will that you should be unduly sad and despondent.
>
> Our enemy tries to depress us by false fears which he proposes. His intention is to make us so weary and dejected, that we let the blessed sight of our everlasting friend slip from our minds.
>
> It is a beautiful humility—brought about by the grace and mercy of the Holy Spirit—when a sinful soul willingly and gladly accepts the chastisement our Lord himself would give us. It will seem light and easy, if only we will accept contentedly what he calls upon us to bear.

The key phrase of the passage is "a beautiful humility." Although it feels as if Julian throws us a curve ball here by tying this lovely phrase to our "willingly and gladly" accepting "the chastisement our Lord himself would give us," perhaps she is suggesting that from such a loving and gracious Lord, receiving correction is more encouraging than discouraging.

I love the kindness in this passage from Julian. She tells us of Jesus' concern about our self-condemnation, "Do not blame yourself too much." She urges us not "to be unduly sad and despondent." She reminds us that Satan seeks to drag us into depression by means of "false fears." She urges us not to allow "the blessed sight of our everlasting friend slip from our minds." Mother Julian offers us much encouragement.

PART III

The Warm Moons

(SUMMER—*BLOKÉTU*)

The Moon When the Berries Are Good

June 18–July 15

If my people who are called by my name humble themselves, pray,
seek my face, and turn from their wicked ways, then I will hear
from heaven, and will forgive their sin and heal their land.

Yahweh (2 Chronicles 7:14)

If God supplies you with some gift, beg him that he might teach you how
this gift can help you progress in humility . . . or else beg him to remove
the gift from you so that it might not become the cause of your downfall.

Isaac of Nineveh

(((((FIRST WEEK)))))

THE FRUIT OF LOVE

The sixth Lakota virtue is *Icicupi*, "sacrifice." Here is how this virtue is described:

> Sacrifice is giving of oneself. The fruit of love is sacrifice. In the beginning the Creator sacrificed itself to make all that there is and through this humble act we can understand the significance of offering ourselves. In order to accomplish anything, one must be able to make a sacrifice. Whether it be the small sacrifices of your daily life or major sacrifices of your

lifetime, we all reap what we sow by this fundamental act. We sacrifice our time and effort every day just to get things done but on a larger spiritual scale we can give of ourselves and give back to the Creator.

"The fruit of love is sacrifice." I genuinely like the tying of love to sacrifice. This understanding is one thing that will keep sacrifice from degenerating into destructive expressions. Love is a well-reasoned concern for the good of all; hence sacrifice that flows from love is life-giving to all.

THREE DISTINCT EXPERIENCES, THREE SIMPLE LESSONS

This morning I leave before sunrise for a hike in the canyon to avoid the heat of the day. On the way I come across a wild mother turkey with five babies in tow. Five. Wow! A new sight for me.

When I arrive at the canyon, I notice that nearly all the early summer wildflowers have now disappeared . . . done in by summer's heat. But I discover two notable exceptions. On the canyon rim the sunflowers are opening up with a burst of yellow petals, which are constantly stretching out toward the sun.

Once down in the canyon I am greeted by a wonderful spread of western spiderwort flowers. These one-inch-wide blossoms are most distinctive. Without fail each blossom has three deep purple petals and in the center are purple stamens that support bright yellow anthers. On hot days these plants will tend to open up in the morning and close down as the afternoon heat comes on. Hence, as I pass by their blossoms are stretching out wide and their purple splendor dominates the landscape.

Three distinct experiences, three simple lessons for the spiritual life. The mother turkey watching over her young is a lesson in sacrifice. The sunflower constantly turning into the light is a lesson for us to be ever turning, turning, turning toward Christ, our true light.

And the royal purple of the western spiderwort is a lesson reminding us of Christ's royal rule among his people.

PAUL'S EXAMPLE OF HUMILITY

Today I am studying Paul's example of humility in his missionary travels. I'm especially taken by his words to the Ephesian elders who he asked to meet him along the coast as he was making his way to Jerusalem. He knew he would not see them again and he told them so. When they gathered, he spoke to them, "You yourselves know how I lived among you the entire time from the first day that I set foot in Asia, serving the Lord *with all humility* and with tears, enduring the trials that came to me" (Acts 20:18-19).

The word Paul uses here is *tapeinophrosynē*, literally "lowliness of mind." I decided to look at some of the other translations I have in my library to see how different translators have handled this word. Above I quoted from the NRSV. Here is the result of my little search of other translations:

- King James Version (KJV)—"Serving the Lord *with all humility of mind*, and with many tears, and temptations, which befell me."

- New English Bible (NEB)—"I served the Lord *in all humility* amid the sorrows and trials that came upon me."

- Phillips—"I have served the Lord *most humbly* and what tears I have shed over the trials that have come to me."

- New International Version (NIV)—"I served the Lord *with great humility* and with tears, although I was severely tested."

- New American Standard Bible (NASB)—"I was with you the whole time, serving the Lord *with all humility* and with tears and with trials."

- Common English Bible (CEB)—"I served the Lord *with great humility* and with tears in the midst of trials that came upon me."

- The Living Bible (TLB)—"I have done the Lord's work *humbly*—yes, and with tears—and have faced grave danger."
- First Nations Version (FNV)—"I did all Creator asked of me *with a humble heart*, as I walked a trail of tears."
- *The Message*—"You know that from day one of my arrival in Asia I was with you totally—*laying my life on the line*, serving the Master no matter what, putting up with no end of scheming."

The paraphrase rendering of *The Message*, "laying my life on the line," adds an interesting dimension to *tapeinophrosynē*. Well, I long for more of this "lowliness of mind" to be manifest in our day.

When Paul finished speaking to the Ephesian elders, we read that "he knelt down with them all and prayed. There was much weeping among them all; they embraced Paul and kissed him, grieving especially because of what he had said, that they would not see him again" (Acts 20:36-38). Such overwhelming love and care they shared with each other. Oh, may our churches today exhibit such love and care.

(((((SECOND WEEK)))))

THE THREEFOLD IMPRINT OF THE SPIRIT

Tonight I am intrigued by Evelyn Underhill's discussion of the three distinguishing characteristics of a life that is acting out of an "immense depth" of God working on the soul: tranquility, gentleness, and strength.

In *The Spiritual Life* Underhill tells us that she is borrowing this insight from Saint John of the Cross, but she unpacks it in ways that are uniquely Evelyn Underhill. She writes, "Tranquility, gentleness, and strength, carry us through the changes of weather, the ups and downs of the route, the varied surface of the road; the inequalities of family life, emotional and professional disappointments, the sudden intervention of bad fortune or bad health, the rising and falling of our religious temperature. This is the threefold imprint of the Spirit on the souls surrendered to His great action."

Now, Underhill is not here writing as someone enclosed and protected in the cloister but as a woman smack in the middle of the push and shove of early-twentieth-century London life.

She continues on to interpret this "threefold imprint of the Spirit" in fuller detail: "Thus there is no tendency to snatch another's work, or dodge dull bits of their own; no cheapening sense of hurry, or nervous anxiety about success. The action of those whose lives are given to the Spirit has in it something of the leisure of Eternity; and because of this, they achieve far more than those whose lives are enslaved by the rush and hurry, the unceasing tick-tick of the world."

"The leisure of Eternity" . . . I know so very little of this divine leisure. Lord, show me, teach me, lead me into such a life.

"Rest, my child, rest. You have nothing to do but to rest. In time I will show you how you can work resting."

THE NARROW TRACK WHICH LEADS UP AND OUT

Underhill next shows us the other side of the coin. At the very time we are discovering the outward marks of tranquility, gentleness, and strength we are also engaged in "the effort and struggle of the interior life." Inwardly we experience "the pain and tension which must be felt by imperfect creatures when they contemplate and stretch towards a beauty and perfection which they cannot reach."

Underhill explains that this "beauty and perfection" is like a magnet drawing us in. This inward journey "means effort, faithfulness, courage, and sometimes grim encounters if [we are] to respond to that attraction, and move towards it along the narrow track which leads up and out from the dark valleys of the mind."

Interesting . . . these seemingly contradictory experiences of outward calm and inward struggle. I'm wondering if perhaps I need to engage in a double search for this summer season. First, watching to see to what extent I actually exhibit the outward marks of tranquility and gentleness and strength. And, at the same time, observing to see to what extent I sense the inner struggle which "draws us out of darkness into His great light."

One question: Should I record everything I am learning or is it better to avoid disclosing private introspection? I'm inclined to hold my pen: some experiences are best kept between God and the soul.

HUMILITY AND HOLINESS ARE TWINS

This morning I decide to secure Andrew Murray's *Humility: The Beauty of Holiness.* Over the years I've read a goodly number of Murray's writings and at least one was on the topic of humility, but this particular linking of humility with holiness felt like a fruitful line of thinking. So, I pulled the trigger and bought it . . . the huge investment of $7.99.

Since I do not have Amazon Prime, I am ordering it via snail mail and it will take a week or so to arrive. I rather favor the delay . . . "instant" material on humility seems a little odd. So, it is yet to arrive, but even before arriving the subtitle stimulates my thinking about the relationship between humility and holiness.

Anyway, as I am waiting for Murray's book, I pick up Thomas Kelly's *A Testament of Devotion.* Even though I have read this slender volume many times I never fail to receive something life-giving from its pages. Randomly I flip to his discussion of "holy obedience" and come upon these words, "The fruits of holy obedience are many. But two are so closely linked together that they can scarcely be treated separately. They are the passion for personal holiness and the sense of utter humility."

Kelly goes on for several pages unpacking the symbiotic relationship of these two. Then he pulls me up short with this surprising assertion: "humility and holiness are twins in the astonishing birth of obedience in the heart."

I am struck to the core. Yes, of course. Kelly is spot on. And this is exactly my Achilles heel. Today I feel far removed from holiness of heart and mind and soul. My thoughts are prodigal, wandering far from God. A line from an old hymn surfaces to my consciousness: "Prone to wander, Lord, I feel it; / Prone to leave the God I love." Yes, that describes me. And then Kelly places his finger right on the remedy: "Growth in humility is a measure of our growth in the habit of the Godward-directed mind."

Then too vanity and human arrogance always look for an opening into the human heart. Kelly exclaims, "O how slick and weasel-like is self-pride!" So, how can we conquer the self-conceit and egoism that eat away at the soul? Kelly again, "Only the utterly humble ones can bow and break the raging pride of a power-mad world."

So, today I pray, "O Lord, purify my heart." Scripture reminds us that the pure in heart shall see God. And Kelly adds, "More, they who see God shall cry out to become pure in heart, even as He is pure, with all the energy of their souls."

May I see God! May I grow into the purity of heart that allows me to see God safely. Today. Tomorrow. All the tomorrows that are in the future.

THE HIGH PLACES

I am continuing to read Jeffrey Ostler's *The Lakotas and the Black Hills: The Struggle for Sacred Ground*. The Black Hills (*He Sapa* to the Lakota) are one of the most extraordinary landscapes of the

Great Plains. Rising four thousand feet above the plains like an immense oval, 120 miles long and 50 miles wide, it is a forested island in a sea of grass. Of course, we today know the area for the giant granite carvings at Mount Rushmore, but many other high places abound: the Cathedral Spires, Black Elk Peak, and a bit northwest is the volcanic neck of the Black Hills known to us today as Devils Tower and to the Lakota as *Mato Tipila*, meaning "Bear Lodge." There is an interesting story behind this Lakota name, but I want to keep my focus on the high places in the Black Hills.

Of supreme importance for the Lakota is that these sites have sacred significance as destinations for young men and women to engage in a "vision quest." As best I understand the Lakota vision quest it involves three core elements.

Solitude. This involves removing oneself from all social interaction, cultural roles, routines, habits and the expectations of others. The individual says farewell to all human authorities—parents, teachers, peer groups, and all social media—and seeks to become attentive to the guidance of the "Great Spirit."

Nature. Whenever possible this is in a wilderness setting so that the individual can focus on returning to intimate relationship with the earth itself. Physically, it means leaving behind roads, houses, and all forms of the humanly created world. Hence, the importance of "the high places" so the individual can enter the older world of nature where the earth can awaken forgotten senses and atrophied ways of perceiving.

Fasting. In fasting the person on a vision quest refrains from the normal function of eating in order to engage in intense spiritual activity. Here the person is open to an encounter with the transcendent, with *Wakan Tanka*, the "Great Spirit," to use Lakota language.

The purpose of the vision quest involves discovering direction, gifts, purpose, and vision for life. Sparrow Hart writes, "In a vision quest, the rules, roles, and routines of normal life are left behind, and—in both simple and profound ways—we experience a resetting of our compass, a renewal of the core truths and commitments that serve to guide us through life."

Listening to and learning from Lakota teaching on the vision quest is an act of humility on our part. To be sure, I would take issue with the pantheistic strands that can be found in the Lakota teaching on the vision quest. But I also want to allow that Christ, who is the true light that enlightens every person coming into the world, will come to honest seekers and bring them light for their journey (Jn 1:9).

(((((THIRD WEEK)))))

A Special Gift

I'm beginning to discover a special gift of humility—a growing ability to be teachable. I'll take this as a great freedom.

This New Double Way of Living

A good word (a prayer really) comes from G. K. Chesterton:

> O God of earth and alter,
> bow down and hear our cry;
> our earthly rulers falter,
> our people drift and die;
> the walls of gold entomb us,
> the swords of scorn divide;
> take not Thy thunder from us,
> but take away our pride.

I am especially taken by the final lines, "take not Thy thunder from us, but take away our pride." The thunder is needed for us to continue going through life with courage against the evils that plague modern society. But we need to learn to do so minus the arrogance and pride that so often accompany "thunder." So, Lord, teach me this new double way of living . . . never surrendering to evil and never rising up in hubris.

THE ABSENCE OF ALL PRETENSE WHATSOEVER

I sit this noon hour in a small café I like to seek out now and again. It is a bit of a distance from where I live. But I take the time to come here because I enjoy the people. This is a rural community, mostly ranchers and farmers. I like to sit and watch the customers, most wearing Levis or overalls . . . hardworking and closely tied to the earth. Now, I don't want to overromanticize—they can swear freely and carry on the heated angers and pettinesses you will find most anywhere.

But what I like here is the absence of all pretense whatsoever. No vanity or strutting. No efforts to impress or show off. It makes me feel comfortable here even though I do not share their lifestyle. They simply accept me at face value. We can talk freely about the weather and the price of grain and a host of trivia. Of course, I mostly listen, for they dwell in a world I can see and understand only from a distance. I can even share with them that I write books (which I seldom do) and they merely nod and say, "That's nice," and quickly return to topics that touch them viscerally. I like this. I enjoy sitting here in an environment free from pretense. It seems to cleanse my soul!

AN UTTER SIMPLICITY

I rise early today and decide to hike in the canyon once there is sufficient light. It is a glorious day with clouds hanging low and an early mist descending and watering the grasses . . . perfect for hiking. I am alone in the canyon except, of course, for the wildlife. In one field I spot a wild turkey, a female. She is by herself, which is rather unusual in my experience; normally, when I see wild turkeys, they are traveling in groupings of a dozen or so.

This female seems oblivious to anybody or anything, slowly scratching and pecking her way through the field. An utter simplicity seems to envelop the scene. I certainly would not want to ascribe the virtue of "humility" to a wild turkey in a field but the scene was completely devoid of any grasping and grabbing for position or status. I watch for a time and as I watch I feel my own grasping and grabbing slowly slipping away.

This is one reason I like coming here. In the woods I sense that the trees and the birds and the creatures of the earth are all doing the will of the Father. The creation has most certainly been affected by the fall; nevertheless, creation continues to reflect back something of the goodness of God. I revel in the goodness of the creation.

TWO VERY DIFFERENT BOOKS

Today I begin reading two very different books on Lakota life and history. The larger book (*Lakota America*, 530 pages) is written by Pekka Hämäläinen, who teaches American history at Oxford. Immediately I could see that this is a serious work of history, but I wonder why someone who hailed from Finland would take up the topic of the Lakota culture, a topic so far removed from his own culture. And I wonder what kind of twist he might give to the subject.

The smaller volume (*The Lakota Way*, 240 pages) is authored by Joseph M. Marshall III, who was born on the Rosebud Rez and whose first language is Lakota. I must say he certainly gained a first-rate mastery of the English language somewhere along the way as his storytelling is wonderfully evocative.

I am immediately drawn into *The Lakota Way*, but I do hope to gain from the approaches of both books. I imagine I will be reading in these two books for several months and hopefully some insights from them will find their way into these pages as I go along.

The Moon When the Chokecherries Are Black

I therefore, the prisoner in the Lord, beg you to lead a life worthy of the calling to which you have been called, with all humility and gentleness, with patience, bearing with one another in love, making every effort to maintain the unity of the Spirit in the bond of peace.

PAUL (EPHESIANS 4:1-3)

Humility of heart is born in a person from two sources: full awareness of one's sins and contemplation on the humility of our Lord.

ISAAC THE SYRIAN

(((((FIRST WEEK)))))

BEING HONEST ABOUT YOURSELF AND THE WORLD AROUND YOU

The seventh Lakota virtue is *Wowicake*, "truth." Here is how this virtue is described: "Truth is being honest about yourself and the world around you."

What a wonderful way to think about this virtue. Honest about myself. Honest about the world around me. That's what I need.

ITKÓMI, THE TRICKSTER

In *The Lakota Way* Joseph Marshall writes, "I asked my grandfather once, when he was in his sixties, . . . if he could tell me what truth was. 'I don't think I've lived long enough to know that,' he said, 'all I know is that without it Iktómi would be the most powerful being on earth.'"

In Lakota lore *Iktómi* is the Trickster who promises an illusive reality but in truth delivers an opposite reality.

Marshall then adds, "We Lakota have heard Iktómi sing several times. At the Fort Laramie Treaty Council of 1851, as thousands upon thousands of white emigrants made their way along the Oregon Trail from Missouri to Oregon and passed through Lakota territory, the United States peace commissioners told us, 'They are only passing through and need only as much room as the width of the wagon wheels.'"

Next Marshall references the Fort Laramie Treaty of 1868 which "established the Great Sioux Reservation—the entire western half of the current state of South Dakota—for 'as long as the sun shall rise, as long as the rivers shall flow, as long as the grasses shall grow.'"

Iktómi, the Trickster, has once again spoken an illusion and run roughshod over the truth.

HUMILITY IN ITS MOST FUNDAMENTAL FORM

I arise at 6:00 a.m. with the hopes of getting on the canyon trail by 7:30. Even so, it is quite warm at the trailhead. I am the second person on the trail this day so it is a solitary hike . . . except for that first person. He is a jogger that takes to these trails at a rather good clip. After half an hour I see him heading toward me. I give him a wide berth and tip my hat to him. For about ten seconds I envy his athletic prowess and wish for it for myself. On the eleventh second reality strikes me: "He is a twenty-something and I am a seventy-something!" Humility, I think, involves recognizing my place in the scheme of things. At seventy-nine I am grateful just to be walking these trails, if even at a slower pace these days.

I decide to take the route that Nate and I took when he was here a couple weeks ago. This adds an extra loop up along the base of the western canyon walls by the cave. I have a special reason for returning to this trail. I am looking for one particular log step that the park service had installed some years back. I do indeed find it.

Two weeks ago as we were hiking up toward the cliff walls I spied this log and saw carved into its side "KKK." I pointed with my trekking pole and groaned in disgust at the white supremacy impulse that is growing in our day. Nate, however, simply reached for the back of my daypack and took out my knife hanging from a carabineer. The knife is old—not used for probably a decade—and had to be quite dull. Regardless he opened it up and without a word started carving out the offensive three letters.

After finishing he commented simply, "Some African American couple might be hiking here and become genuine frightened by what . . . or who . . . might be out in these woods." Exactly! I had looked at that log and saw only offense. Nate looked and saw the potential for pain, fear, and the wounding of human relationship.

Indeed. What Nate did was totally instinctive . . . a quiet example of service to others. I rather think this is humility in its most fundamental form.

(((((SECOND WEEK)))))

The Story of No Moccasins

I was surprised to learn that Joseph Marshall's book *The Lakota Way* is organized around the twelve Lakota virtues, humility being the first. Marshall opens the book with the lovely story of "No Moccasins," a brave and wise Lakota woman who in the end is distinguished for her humility.

No Moccasins lived before the coming of the horses—that is, prior to 1700. Originally her name was "Carries the Fire" and she certainly put the fire into the heart of a young warrior of sterling reputation by the name of Three Horns. After proper Lakota courtship, Carries the Fire and Three Horns are married, have children and grandchildren, and live into old age. By her sixty-seventh winter No Moccasins' "hair was the color of new-fallen snow" and "the lines in her face seemed to show the many trails she had walked in her life."

But now for the reason for her name change. It is a story that had never been told until Three Horns, at seventy winters, was nearing death. Many had come to pay him honor and he asks the elders—both men and women—to come to his lodge. Once everyone is gathered, he requests the elders to share the story he is about to tell them in all the campfires in the village. He then proceeds to tell how "Carries the Fire" became "No Moccasins."

As a young man Three Horns had gone with five other warriors to rescue two young women who had been captured by an opposing raiding party. Moving quickly they track the raiding party south for half a moon into a land unknown to Three Horns. Finally they catch up with the raiding party just as they were arriving at their village. Three Horns and his companions devise an ingenious rescue plan which works perfectly . . . with the single exception that Three Horns is captured. The other five warriors assume Three Horns has been killed in the rescue raid and in great haste they returned north to their village with the heartbreaking news about Three Horns to Carries the Fire.

Carries the Fire grieves bitterly for her husband . . . but somehow, even strangely, she begins to doubt the account of Three Horns' death. So, she learns where the enemies' village is located and late one night she dresses in her husband's clothes, slips out of the village unnoticed, and makes the long and dangerous journey to the enemy camp.

Meanwhile, the enemy tribe takes out their rage . . . and embarrassment . . . at the successful rescue of the Lakota women on Three Horns. He is reduced to a cruel slavery. By day he is forced to drag poles like a dog until his hands and knees are bleeding. By night his hands and feet are tightly bound and stretched between two stout poles. Three Horns admits, "I began to feel lower than a dung beetle."

Three Horns says, "One night it was cold and rainy, and I was naked and shivering. There was no one about; it was too cold. Even the dogs curled up out of the rain. My heart was sad as I thought about my young wife and that I would never, ever see her again. I thought about her so much that her face appeared to me. After a moment I realized it was real; she was there! While I lay there in disbelief she cut my bonds with her knife, pulled me to my feet, and guided me out of the enemy's village."

With the rain covering their tracks they walk quickly through the night. By dawn they arrive at a hiding place Carries the Fire has prepared for them. They hide there and eat and rest until Three Horns regains some of his strength.

Cautiously Carries the Fire and Three Horns start back home knowing that a party of the enemy's best warriors is hunting for them. Finally, they hide in an old bear's den to allow Three Horns a chance to rest. As he sleeps Carries the Fire slips out, returning that evening soaking wet and barefoot. She had placed her moccasins near a creek to lay a false trail for their pursuers. Almost being spotted she slips into the creek and hides inside a beaver lodge.

Upon returning to their village days later Carries the Fire refuses to allow Three Horns to tell their story, only allowing him to say that he had escaped from his captors. But Three Horns does give her a new name, "No Moccasins," never explaining the reason for it.

But now, around his lodge fire he at last shares with the elders the story behind her new name.

Three Horns concludes by saying, "I have known good people in my life. Many were wise, honorable, generous, and brave. But none, except this old woman who sits beside me as always, had the one strength that gives true meaning to all the others—humility."

The Burden of Humility Is Light

In concluding the story of No Moccasins, Marshall observes, "The burden of humility is light because a truly humble person divests himself or herself of the need for recognition. The burden of arrogance, on the other hand, grows heavier day by day. In sharing the journey of life, travel with the humble person on the quiet path."

I love this story of No Moccasins because it takes me in a direction I hadn't expected. I had been expecting that Three Horns would be held up as the prime example of humility—yet as it turned out, his wife was the one praised. How delightful, and how instructive for our patriarchal culture.

Jesus' Masculinity

Historian Kristin Kobes Du Mez has written a challenging book titled *Jesus and John Wayne*. It is actually a study in masculinity and she takes special aim at evangelicals' efforts to define Christian men as "rugged, aggressive GI Joes for Jesus."

Commenting on *Jesus and John Wayne*, Episcopal priest Noah Van Niel notes that this way of defining masculinity leaves out central elements of Jesus' masculinity like "compassion, humility and purpose." Discussing humility he writes, "Jesus doesn't use his power to show off or control others; he rejects Satan's offer of the splendors of the world. His power is for the powerless, made great by being given away. To the poor, the oppressed, and the persecuted he proclaims, 'Yours is the kingdom of heaven.'" Van Neil argues that Jesus' masculinity shows us how to "renounce the drive for supremacy and dominance, stop glorifying our own strength and authority, and pursue humility and service, lifting up others, not ourselves."

Kobes Du Mez and Van Niel are spot on. But, so often, I too am attracted to the tough-guy machismo found in so much of contemporary culture . . . even contemporary religious culture. My heart becomes hardened against a masculinity that would stress "compassion, humility, and purpose."

May I learn a new way, a Jesus way, as I seek to live with family and friends and neighbors. And, yes, even enemies. Teach me this new way, dear Lord.

(((((THIRD WEEK)))))

THE TRIAD OF QUALITIES

Ephesians 4:2 is a familiar passage to me, but this afternoon it struck me in a new way as I encountered it in the NIV, "Be completely humble and gentle; be patient, bearing with one another in love." Maybe it's the triad of qualities that caught my attention . . . "humble" . . . "gentle" . . . "patient" . . . combined with the defining phrase, "bearing with one another in love." Anyway, I think I shall memorize this passage, writing it out on a three-by-five card and carrying it with me for perhaps a month, and see if there are ways it might enhance my understanding of humility.

GOD WATCHES OVER THE HUMBLE PERSON

This afternoon I am sitting with Thomas à Kempis's marvelous book, *The Imitation of Christ*. I am using the William Creasy translation that I find the most satisfying. I've just turned to book two, chapter two and come upon a meaningful discussion of humility. I have underlined parts of it from past readings, but I don't remember it. It instructs me exactly where I need help these days in allowing others to observe my faults. Even more, Thomas draws me in close to understand how much God watches over the humble person.

The passage is best quoted in full:

> The fact that others know our faults and disapprove of them is often a great help in deepening our humility. When a person humbles himself for his failings he easily satisfies others and he appeases those who are angry with him. God protects and delivers a humble person; he cherishes and consoles him. God gives himself to a humble person; he bestows great grace on him, and after his humiliation he raises him to glory. God reveals his secrets to those who are humble, and he sweetly draws them and calls them to himself. The humble person in the midst of trouble is filled with peace, for he depends on God alone. Do not think that you have made any progress unless you feel truly humble before God and others.

Right now I am struck by the concluding sentence: "Do not think that you have made any progress unless you feel truly humble before God and others." What a marker for progress in the spiritual life! I'm going to have to live with this statement for a while.

HUMILITY AND *OTIUM SANCTUM*

I am wondering if there is a connection between humility and what the devotional masters described as *otium sanctum*, holy leisure. In holy leisure we are set free from the need to control, to push, to earn, to achieve. Holy leisure refers to a sense of balance in life, an ability to be at peace throughout the activities of the day, an ability to rest and take time to enjoy beauty, an ability to slow down and enter the cosmic patience of God.

When people try to define us only by what we produce it takes a deep humility of spirit to move in another direction. Humility gives us the strength to turn from "the frantic scramble of panting feverishness" we see all around us and instead quietly enter *otium sanctum,* holy leisure.

THE FINEST FLOWERING OF HUMAN VIRTUE

Way back in 1908 W. S. Bruce in *The Formation of Christian Character* wrote, "The Christian man [he means "human being"] is man *at his highest moral efficiency.* He is the man with the richest ethical experience. Christian graces are the finest flowering of human virtue. When the Spirit of God begins to quicken and nourish the roots of piety, obligation becomes joyous service, and duty changes its name to delight."

This reality is so seldom seen in our lived experience because we have so often divorced "Christian" from "character." We no longer think in terms of the Christian becoming like Christ. Bruce unpacks this problem in careful detail and then directs us to confess, "I hope yet to be like Him, and to see Him as He is." In so doing, Bruce says, the Christian "feels the power of the moral imperative to purify himself 'even as He is pure.'"

In this way, says Bruce, "ethics receives a new baptism. It gives to all virtuous activity stability, encouragement, and permanence." The virtues "give firmness to . . . the fabric of Christian character."

Yes, indeed. And for the follower of Jesus humility is first among the virtues.

THE GREAT EQUALIZER

Today, I went to the memorial service for Larry Crabb. A moving service on multiple levels. The experience causes me to reflect on death as the great equalizer. It comes to us all. It overtakes the powerful just as surely as the impotent, the famous as surely as the obscure, the strong as surely as the weak, the rich as surely as the poor. To say "death happens" would not make a peppy bumper sticker. But, say it we must . . . it happens to me . . . it happens to us all . . . death happens.

But for the follower of the Way death does not have the last say. Through the power of Jesus' life, death, and resurrection, our death is ultimately defeated:

> Death has been swallowed up in victory.
> Where, O death, is your victory?
> Where, O death, is your sting? . . .
> thanks be to God, who gives us the victory through our
>   Lord Jesus Christ. (1 Cor 15:54-57)

I sit throughout the service quiet and pensive. It is moving to consider the reality of my death and the death of all those sitting around me. But how much more moving to contemplate the ultimate defeat of death in Jesus Christ, our Lord. It is a humbling reality.

(((((FOURTH WEEK)))))

WISDOM AND HUMILITY

Is there a connection between wisdom and humility? When we have thoughtful reflection on our multiple experiences in life—both good and bad—it provides us with knowledge. But knowledge, by itself, is not wisdom. So, how do we move from knowledge to wisdom? I'll think on it for a while.

MASSIVE AMOUNTS OF HUMILITY

When we thoughtfully apply the knowledge that comes through years of experience, we learn ways to overcome our arrogance and impatience and willfulness and anger . . . the list could go on for some time. In *The Lakota Way* Joseph Marshall writes,

> Life demands that we exercise perseverance, face adversity with courage, demonstrate fortitude in the midst of temptation, tell the truth no matter how painful, walk in humility, sacrifice for our families, practice generosity to be truly rich, respect all who are part of the Great Circle of Life, choose honor above personal gain, act with compassion toward the needy, strive for harmony in personal relationships, and otherwise demonstrate the virtues that give meaning to life.

When we make these life-giving choices, it allows us to travel from knowledge into wisdom. Wisdom is choosing the right thing to say and do . . . at the right time . . . in the right place . . . and with the right inner motivation. For us to be able to exercise wisdom in this way requires that we possess massive amounts of humility.

HUMILITY CONTENDS WITH GREATER ENEMIES

In my early search for resources to help me understand how the heart, mind, body, and soul can be formed into the likeness of Christ, I soon realized that a Great Conversation had been going on for centuries on this very subject. One of my early discoveries was a book by William Law (1686–1761) under the rather foreboding title *A Serious Call to a Devout and Holy Life*.

Bonhoeffer's *Cost of Discipleship* was actually my very first exposure to genuine Christian discipleship. For me it was a goldmine and kept me in the faith throughout my teen years. William Law and his *Serious Call* came next. What this book did is

hard to calculate. For me it enlarged and deepened my understanding of "devotion," taking it out of merely a pious exercise and
placing it squarely in daily life and daily activities.

A *Serious Call* is not a quick read. I have been in and out of it for
decades. The other day I came across an insight into humility which
I had never seen before . . . or if I had seen it, I paid scant attention.
But this morning the words gripped my heart and awakened my
spirit. Here is Law in his own words: "Lastly, courage and bravery
are words of a great sound and seem to signify a heroic spirit; but
yet humility, which seems to be the lowest, meanest part of devotion, is a more certain argument of a noble and courageous mind.
For humility contends with greater enemies, is more constantly
engaged, more violently assaulted, bears more, suffers more, and
requires greater courage to support itself than any instances of
worldly bravery."

LET EVERY DAY BE A DAY OF HUMILITY

One final teaching on humility from *A Serious Call*. Like the old
writers were known to do, Law includes a rather long sentence of
forty-eight words . . . so we need to be patient in unpacking it: "Let
every day . . . be a day of humility. Condescend to all the weakness
and infirmities of your fellow creatures, cover their frailties, love
their excellencies, encourage their prosperities, compassionate
their distress, receive their friendship, overlook their unkindness,
forgive their malice, be a servant of servants, and condescend to
the lowest offices to the lowest of mankind."

The Moon of the Harvest

AUGUST 13–SEPTEMBER 9

I will bless the LORD at all times;
his praise shall continually be in my mouth.
My soul makes its boast in the LORD;
let the humble hear and be glad.
O magnify the LORD with me,
and let us exalt his name together.

DAVID (PSALM 34:1-3)

It is neither asceticism nor vigils nor any other work
which saves us; only sincere humility.

THEODORA, A MOTHER OF THE DESERT

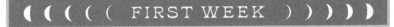

(((((FIRST WEEK)))))

THE UNCONDITIONAL LOVE THAT
CREATES TRUE COMPASSION

The eighth Lakota virtue is *Waunsilapi*, "compassion," which is described like this: "Doing what is right in caring for others as you would yourself is what makes a person compassionate. One need not feel sorry for or sympathetic to anyone in order to live this virtue. In fact it is that inner strength that allows us to have the unconditional love that creates true compassion."

This description of compassion brings to my mind that wonderful biblical passage about what is good and what the Lord requires of us: "to do justice, and to love kindness, and to walk humbly with your God" (Mic 6:8). That is all . . . that is enough.

I certainly could use more of this "true compassion." In our day we see lots of "compassion" that is not true compassion; rather it becomes efforts to boost our own standing in life. Lord Jesus, increase in me more of this "unconditional love that creates true compassion."

THE HYMN USED AT OUR WEDDING

Last night I decided on an early morning hike in the canyon in order to avoid the heat of the day. As it turned out I rose before the dawn's daylight had come. As I wait for the light which proceeds the dawn I thumb through an old hymnal, and quite by accident I come upon the hymn that was used at our wedding fifty-four years ago, "Come, Thou Fount of Every Blessing." I quickly photocopy it and stuff it in my pocket.

Once the light of the day begins to come on, I leave, arriving at the canyon before sunrise. I am the first in the canyon today, so I make my way to a little amphitheater of log benches overlooking Pike's Peak—"Sun Mountain" to the Ute people.

Alone, I sing the hymn, each verse taking me back to our highly anticipated wedding day so many years ago:

Come thou Fount of every blessing,
Tune my heart to sing thy grace;
Streams of mercy, never ceasing,
Call for songs of loudest praise.
Teach me some melodious sonnet,
Sung by flaming tongues above;
Praise the mount! I'm fixed upon it,
Mount of thy redeeming love.
Here I raise mine Ebenezer;

Hither by thy help I'm come;
And I hope, by thy good pleasure,
Safely to arrive at home.
Jesus sought me when a stranger,
Wandering from the fold of God;
He, to rescue me from danger,
Interposed his precious blood.
O to grace how great a debtor
Daily I'm constrained to be!
Let thy goodness like a fetter,
Bind my wandering heart to thee:
Prone to wander, Lord I feel it,
Prone to leave the God I love;
Here's my heart, O take and seal it,
Seal it for thy courts above. Amen.

I then proceed on my hike with the words of the hymn ringing in my mind and the music of the hymn in my heart. It makes for a good hike. I finish tired of body but bright in spirit.

YEARS OF SLOW, PAINFUL UNSELFING

Today I am reading a manuscript by author Paula Huston titled *The Hermits of Big Sur*. Extremely well-written and thoughtful. It explores the contemplative tradition through the lens of one particular community, New Camaldoli Hermitage, situated in the beautiful Big Sur hills overlooking the Pacific.

In my reading I came upon an insight from Huston that connects with my exploration into humility: "You do not become a contemplative overnight. In fact, to become holy and full of wisdom in this way requires years of slow, painful unselfing. Desires must be dealt with. Passions must be tamed. The mind must be trained. Humility must become second nature, a way of life. The Christian monastic tradition calls the outcome of this unselfing process *puritas cordis,* or purity of heart."

Of course, my concern is to deepen my understanding of how this "unselfing" works in ordinary life. How can humility "become second nature, a way of life" for me smack in the middle of appointments and phone calls and the multiplied demands of daily life? Is it possible to experience a genuine unselfing here? These are the kinds of questions I hope to answer.

The contemplative tradition reminds us that seasons of solitude and silence are essential elements in the recipe for any genuine formation of heart and mind and soul. My heart yearns to see more of the fruit of unselfing in everyday experience.

(((((SECOND WEEK)))))

A PRAYER OF HUMILITY

Today I have been meditating on a rather strange passage in the Hebrew Scriptures . . . the story of Jabez. His story takes up only two verses and there is no further mention of Jabez anywhere in the Bible. Here is the brief text: "Jabez was honored more than his brothers; and his mother named him Jabez, saying, 'Because I bore him in pain.' Jabez called on the God of Israel, saying, 'Oh that you would bless me and enlarge my border, and that your hand might be with me, and that you would keep me from hurt and harm!' And God granted what he asked" (1 Chron 4:9-10).

In Hebrew this passage is a play on the word *pain.* The word *jabez* means "borne in pain," his mother evidently naming him this because of the exceeding difficult experience she went through with his birth. I rather imagine Jabez suffered considerably from this name, ridiculed and teased by the other children mercilessly.

Some years back there was quite a stir over this prayer from a book written about it. Unfortunately, it became all tangled up in prosperity theology and missed the central point of the prayer.

This, in reality, is a prayer of humility. In this simple prayer Jabez is asking to be liberated from the consequences of his birth and his name. And I am impressed with the scriptural economy of words in describing the result of this humble prayer, "And God granted what he asked." Wonderful.

STICKING CLOSE TO THE ROOT

I am sitting again with Thomas Kelly's discussion of "Humility and Holiness" in *A Testament of Devotion*. Today he captures me with his double definition . . . first what humility is not and then what it is: "Humility does not rest, in final count, upon bafflement and discouragement and self-disgust at our shabby lives, a brow-beaten, dog-slinking attitude. It rests upon the disclosure of the consummate wonder of God, upon finding that only God counts, that all our own self-originated intentions are works of straw. And so in lowly humility we must stick close to the Root."

I'm wondering about his insistence on "sticking close to the Root." He is declaring unambiguously that the closer we grow toward God the deeper our humility. In another place he writes, "humility rests upon a holy-blindedness" . . . blinded to all other loyalties, only God alone.

Well, I am so very far from this. My loyalties are divided. I feel fractured and fragmented . . . no, I am fractured and fragmented. Purify my heart, O God. Renew my mind. Sanctify my imagination. Enlarge my soul.

I am encouraged by Kelly's statement further on that "growth in humility is a measure of our growth in the habit of the Godward-directed mind." Developing a "habit" of a "Godward-directed mind" . . . that is something I can work on.

A Quiet Humility

Today we need to bring down five trees on our acreage. We have hundreds of fine Black Forest pines here and we watch over them carefully. These five have not survived the winter, and in our concern for fire mitigation they need to be removed.

I mourn a little every time a tree comes down. These trees have become my friends. I have even named some of them. In honor of the Victor Hugo novel I have dubbed one tree near the house "The Hunchback of Notre Dame" for its twisted hump, bent over but strong and growing. One weathered tree that is clearly the oldest and largest on the property I have named "Treebeard" in honor of J. R. R. Tolkien's primeval Ents, trees who are the ancient shepherds of the forest. Carolynn named one tree after me, and I can sit out on our deck in the morning and watch it grow. Indeed, I watch them all grow for in their growing they are all doing the will of the Father.

This morning from the deck I am watching Robert cut down our five dead trees. I marvel at his skills. Long ago I did a little chainsaw work . . . but once I cut into my own boot with the chainsaw, my foot being saved only by the steel shank in my boot. That abruptly ended my chainsaw cutting days!

So, I am transfixed by Robert's expertise with the winch, the chainsaw, the chipper, etc. He is a firefighter by profession and he seems right at home here in our woods, going about his work quickly and efficiently. There is a quiet humility in Robert that I admire.

(((((THIRD WEEK)))))

Both, From Different Angles, Teach Us

I am today thinking about different examples of humility in the New Testament. Jesus, of course, is the paradigm by which we conjugate all the verbs of humility. But there are so many other examples.

I think I would choose Mary as the example par excellence for deep humility of spirit. I'm thinking of her encounter with the angel. The angel's message had to have been shattering to the young teenager . . . her, Mother of Messiah?! And Mary's response is as pure a definition of humility we will find anywhere: "Here am I, the servant of the Lord; let it be with me according to your word" (Lk 1:38). What a lovely expression of the spirit of humility!

And Joseph. We do not have a single word spoken by Joseph in our New Testament. With Mary we have her marvelous "Magnificat": "My soul magnifies the Lord . . ." (Lk 1:46-55). But with Joseph there is no speech, no declarations, no words at all . . . simply humble obedience. When Joseph learns of Mary's pregnancy he is "unwilling to expose her to public disgrace," and so he "planned to dismiss her quietly" (Mt 1:19). But then an angel of the Lord also visits him, this time in a dream. Having learned the true nature of Mary's situation we read of his act of humility. "When Joseph awoke from sleep, he did as the angel of the Lord commanded him; he took her as his wife, but had no marital relations with her until she had borne a son; and he named him Jesus" (Mt 1:24-25). A lovely act of humble obedience.

I like them both . . . Mary and Joseph. Both, from different angles, teach us about humility.

THE FLOWERS ARE FOR OUR SOULS

I am taken by the Lakota sense of beauty. It focuses quite naturally on aspects of beauty in nature. Kent Nerburn, editor of *The Wisdom of the Native Americans*, is an internationally recognized artist and so he is especially sensitive to the Native American expressions of beauty in nature. He observes their keen attention to the natural beauty of the earth. "I have seen in our midsummer celebrations cool arbors built of fresh-cut branches for council and dance halls, while those who attended decked themselves with leafy boughs, carrying shields and fans of the same, and even making wreaths for their horses' necks. But, strange to say, they seldom make free use of flowers. I once asked the reason for this."

"Why," said one, "the flowers are for our souls to enjoy; not for our bodies to wear. Leave them alone and they will live out their lives and reproduce themselves as the Great Gardener intended. He planted them; we must not pluck them, for it would be selfish to do so."

Stripped Inch by Inch of Self-Importance

This morning I am reading an essay on the radical spiritual vision of Clare of Assisi. One sentence struck me: "She [Clare] embodied Christian truth . . . as one who inch by inch was stripped of self-importance and earthly contrivances until there was nothing left except the skin and bone of her life lived out on an uncomfortable bed." What a powerful description of Christian humility at its zenith . . . being stripped inch by inch of self-importance.

O Lord, help me to enter this way of living that is free of self-importance. But, please, I ask that you *not* bring me into such a reality by hurricane force; rather lead me into this way "inch by inch." Thank you. Amen.

(((((FOURTH WEEK)))))

A Noose That Strangles Humility

For some days I have been puzzling over the meaning of a Lakota proverb. The proverb is simple enough: "Poverty is a noose that strangles humility and breeds disrespect for God and man." But why is it humility (of all the virtues) that is strangled by poverty? And what is it about poverty that strangles humility? On and on.

I am sure there is more for me to learn from this proverb but here is the understanding I have at present. All the virtues, and most especially humility, involve constant practice and attention. Poverty simply blots out all this focus. With poverty the overpowering questions are, "How will I find food for today?" and, "Where will I sleep tonight?" Questions of bare existence dominate everything!

Well, not always. Among the poor we discover virtuous souls . . . souls that exhibit deep humility of heart. I think of Viktor Frankl and Corrie ten Boom, both survivors of the Nazi concentration camps. They, and others like them, shine as beacons of light in a dark, dark place.

Still, the proverb is a reminder of the destructive character of poverty and how it can shrivel the human soul.

WOOD AND FIRE TEACHING HUMILITY

I am beginning to feel that wood and fire must have an interest in teaching humility! Nate decided to climb "Sun Mountain"—that is the Ute name. Most today know it as Pike's Peak. He wanted to climb it from the backside using Craig's Trail.

Well, I decide to help out. So, we tent camp near the trailhead. As the evening comes I build a fire. This I enjoy doing very much. First, I make a small teepee of kindling, adding larger sticks at just the right time, then finally logs until a good steady fire is burning, warming us through the evening. Often I stir the fire, keeping it burning just right. There is nothing more satisfying than cooking dinner over hot flames and simple conversation around warm coals until bedtime.

I enter the tent ready for bed . . . but soon I begin freezing, forgetting how cold it can get at ten thousand feet. All through the night my feet never get warm, so I arise early (maybe 4:30 a.m.) and build another fire. Ah, how satisfying is a hot blaze on a frosty morning.

I walk with Nate to the trailhead and wave goodbye . . . my days of hiking up Fourteeners are behind me. Later I drive around to the front side of Sun Mountain at Manitou Springs and take the Cog Railway to the top. Nate has made the climb in time to take the train down the mountain with me, just as we planned.

We drive back around the mountain to our campsite just in time for me to fix another fire for cooking supper and evening conversation. I gather the kindling and logs just right for the perfect blaze. Again, everything works exactly according to plan. I warm my feet by the fire until they are toasty warm, just right for protecting my feet from freezing through the night. At 6:00 a.m. or so I'm up and ready to build our final fire before breaking camp. But this time, on the fourth fire of our trip, I am in for a humbling surprise.

I arrange the leftover kindling in perfect teepee shape and strike the match. A fire springs up burning brightly . . . and then it begins to smolder. Ugh. I rearrange the small sticks and work more diligently at my small fire. It blazes up, burns for a short time, and then begins smoking heavily and ultimately goes out. "Probably we drenched the embers last night too much," I muse.

So, I go at it again . . . and again . . . and again. By now Nate is up and takes his try at it. Same result. I take over again, concerned now to preserve my reputation as "the keeper of the fire." The results are all meager and by now I have run out of kindling and have only a few larger logs left. We make do with a smoky fire to cook our breakfast. Eating around a smoldering fire we consider that the wood and the fire must have a mind of their own and that, whenever we begin to feel our superiority, the wood and the fire are there to teach us a lesson in humility!

PATIENCE AND HUMILITY

This afternoon I am considering the relationship between patience and humility. The context is common enough. I call a company to arrange for an appointment. The recorded message is always the same. They are so glad I called, they assure me that my call is important to them, they tell me how wonderful their company is, and they assure me that someone will be with me soon. Then I must endure annoying music for ninety seconds . . . and then the recording starts in again. Same message: my call is important to them, their company is the best anywhere, and someone will be with me soon. Then the ear-deafening music again . . . if you can call it music. After twenty minutes of this I hang up frustrated and ready to curse the personless voice on the other end.

That is with a good call. There is also the other kind that forces me to go through a full menu of options, none of which fit my needs . . . and never, ever allows me to actually talk to a human being. I quickly learn that I utterly lack the patience it takes to work my way through our modern techno phone maze. Plus, I am frustrated by the abuse of people's time and energy this system produces.

Patience and humility. They are, I think, cousins in the pantheon of virtues. I have decided that my patience quota is low indeed.

PART IV

The Moons of Change

(AUTUMN—*PTANYÉTU*)

The Moon of the Brown Leaves

SEPTEMBER 10–OCTOBER 7

Truly I tell you, unless you change and become like children,
you will never enter the kingdom of heaven. Whoever becomes
humble like this child is the greatest in the kingdom of heaven.

JESUS (MATTHEW 18:3-4)

The safe and true way to heaven is made by humility,
which lifts up the heart to the Lord, not against Him.

AUGUSTINE OF HIPPO

(((((FIRST WEEK)))))

THIS OPEN ACT OF VULNERABILITY

The ninth Lakota virtue is *Woohitike*, "bravery." It is described this way: "Bravery is born of the wisdom of life and death as well as one's honor. It is not blind or reckless and can come from the very depths of our being in times of need. This open act of vulnerability despite circumstances can help us defy even the worst odds."

I am taken with the Lakota description of bravery as an "open act of vulnerability." This places the emphasis on our need to stand firm for truth and justice rather than attacking others. Anyway, it provides me with a helpful perspective on this Lakota virtue.

I'm wondering . . . in our day and in our culture is living humbly an act of bravery? This might be a fruitful line of thinking.

Your Sister Humility

Last night I asked Carolynn for an old CD of worship music by John Michael Talbot, *Troubadour of the Great King*. I played it as a preparation for sleep, and just as I was gently slipping into sleep I heard the song "The Praises of the Virtues" in which Talbot celebrates "Sister Humility," emphasizing that no one "can live in virtue, without dying unto himself."

A nice way to enter into the sleep.

The Litany of Humility

For several days now I have been living with "The Litany of Humility," commonly attributed to Rafael Cardinal Merry del Val (1865–1930). I am experiencing mixed feelings about this litany . . . a matter I will come to in good time. The one thing I genuinely do appreciate is that this litany views humility as a virtue that we need to seek after intently. What a refreshing contrast from the normal religious sentiment that humility is simply something that will fall on our head . . . that is, if it is even seen as a good thing, which, today it often is not.

Normally a litany is for private devotion and not used in public liturgical worship. It is a form of prayer that contains a repeated responsive petition. Here is the litany in full, including parts that provoke my ambivalence:

The Litany of Humility

O Jesus! Meek and humble of heart, *Hear me.*
From the desire of being esteemed, *Deliver me, Jesus.*
From the desire of being loved, *Deliver me, Jesus.*
From the desire of being extolled, *Deliver me, Jesus.*

From the desire of being honored, *Deliver me, Jesus.*

From the desire of being praised, *Deliver me, Jesus.*

From the desire of being preferred, *Deliver me, Jesus.*

From the desire of being consulted, *Deliver me, Jesus.*

From the desire of being approved, *Deliver me, Jesus.*

From the fear of being humiliated, *Deliver me, Jesus.*

From the fear of being despised, *Deliver me, Jesus.*

From the fear of suffering rebukes, *Deliver me, Jesus.*

From the fear of being calumniated, *Deliver me, Jesus.*

From the fear of being forgotten, *Deliver me, Jesus.*

From the fear of being ridiculed, *Deliver me, Jesus.*

From the fear of being wronged, *Deliver me, Jesus.*

From the fear of being suspected, *Deliver me, Jesus.*

That others may be loved more than I, *Jesus, grant me the grace to desire it.*

That others may be esteemed more than I, *Jesus, grant me the grace to desire it.*

That in the opinion of the world, others may increase and I may decrease, *Jesus, grant me the grace to desire it.*

That others may be praised and I unnoticed, *Jesus, grant me the grace to desire it.*

That others may be preferred to me in everything, *Jesus, grant me the grace to desire it.*

That others may become holier than I, provided that I may become as holy as I should, *Jesus, grant me the grace to desire it.*

(((((SECOND WEEK)))))

THE WISE RESPONSE OF C. S. LEWIS

I appreciate the response of C. S. Lewis to "The Litany of Humility" when it was sent to him by Don Giovanni Calabria. In a letter dated March 27, 1948, Lewis writes, "For the Litany composed by Cardinal Merry many thanks. You did not know, did you, that all the temptations against which he pours forth these prayers I have long been exceeding conscious of? [*From the longing to be thought well of, deliver me, Jesus, . . . from the fear of being rejected, deliver me, Jesus, . . .*] *Touché*, you pink me! Let us pray for each other always. Farewell."

How very wise. Lewis singles out the two besetting temptations against humility that plague the human condition ("the longing to be thought well of" and "the fear of being rejected"). He then embraces them as temptations he himself deals with and welcomes mutual prayer for each another.

A BIT OVERDONE

There are so many of the petitions in "The Litany of Humility" that speak to my condition. It is most certainly worth paying attention to. And, it clearly reflects a good heart. But for me it feels a bit overdone. Studying it and interacting with it is fine. Still, I have trouble every time I try to pray it.

For me it feels like a groveling, almost beggarly form of religious piety. It seems to degrade the glory of the human person made in the image of God. It reminds me of the "worm theology" that I disliked so much as a college student.

Are all desires wrong? What about Augustine's notion of "rightly ordered desires"? Is the desire to be loved by our spouse or our children wrong? Should I really pray "That others may be loved more than I"? And so forth. Well, I think I will take the good I find here and leave the rest.

A Type of Cultural Pluralism

I am very much taken with Ohiyesa (pronounced *Oh hee' yay suh*), meaning "The Winner," a Santee Lakota born in a buffalo hide tipi near Redwood Falls, Minnesota, in the winter of 1858. What interests me is how Ohiyesa bridged both Native American life and Anglo culture in many areas of his life, including religion and spirituality.

As a child Ohiyesa experienced what American history books describe as the "Sioux Uprising of 1862," where he became separated from his father and siblings and assumed they had all been killed. With the remaining members of the Santee Lakota band he was taken into exile in Manitoba, Canada. It is here he was schooled in Lakota spirituality, which he would later write about in *The Soul of the Indian.*

Just as Ohiyesa was entering Lakota manhood at fifteen his father reappeared and sought to bring Ohiyesa with him to a homestead in Flandreau, Dakota Territory, where he along with other Native Americans had moved and had adapted to white culture.

His father made Ohiyesa attend the mission school. We today are keenly aware of the abuses of these mission schools with their operating principle to "kill the Indian and save the man." And, indeed, Ohiyesa was forced to cut his long hair and take an Anglo name, Charles Eastman. In spite of the harsh abuses at the mission school, Ohiyesa/Eastman applied himself diligently to his studies. Two years later he would walk the 150 miles to Santee, Nebraska, to attend a stronger school where he excelled. In time he received his bachelor of science degree from Dartmouth College and in 1890 his MD from Boston University—the first Native American to receive a medical degree.

His first assignment was as "government physician" for the Lakota people at the Pine Ridge Reservation in South Dakota. Here he witnessed the Ghost Dance rebellion of 1890–1891. Later he cared for the Lakota wounded following the massacre at Wounded Knee.

Over his lifetime Ohiyesa/Eastman wrote eleven books. In *The Soul of the Indian*, he articulated the position that his adopted Christian faith was fundamentally compatible with his traditional Lakota spirituality. "We know that all religious aspiration, all sincere worship, can have but one source and goal," he wrote. "We know that the God of the educated and the God of the child, the God of the civilized and the God of the primitive, is after all the same God; and that this God does not measure our differences, but embraces all who live rightly and humbly on the earth."

Such a view was highly controversial in that day, a reality Ohiyesa knew quite well: "They [the missionaries] branded us as pagans and devil-worshipers, and demanded that we renounce our gods as false. They even told us that we were eternally lost unless we adopted their faith and all its symbols."

(((((THIRD WEEK)))))

My Own Take on This Matter

Not only was Ohiyesa's approach highly controversial in his own day; it is, in certain circles, highly controversial today as overly syncretistic. Allow me to venture my own take on this matter.

Jesus Christ is the true light that enlightens every person coming into the world. As the Logos, Jesus is present everywhere and is not blotted out or overwhelmed by the powers of darkness (Jn 1:5-9). Jesus, the Christ, has been at work in all peoples and all cultures . . .

whether they know him or not. As the wise apostle Paul put it, "When Gentiles, who do not possess the law, do instinctively what the law requires, these, though not having the law, are a law to themselves. They show that what the law requires is written on their hearts, . . . and their conflicting thoughts will accuse or perhaps excuse them on the day when, according to my gospel, God, through Jesus Christ, will judge the secret thoughts of all" (Rom 2:14-16).

So, in every culture and people group we look for those areas that are "consonant" with the gospel of Jesus. These we rejoice in and accept as marks of the Spirit. Those areas in the culture that are "disconsonant" with the gospel of Jesus we gladly turn from.

Of course, this places on us a deep burden of discerning the difference between what is consonant with the way of Jesus and what is not. And, this discernment process cuts both ways. We welcome those areas in our own culture that are consonant with the gospel of Jesus, and we turn from those areas that are disconsonant with the gospel of Jesus.

WHY WE NEED CHRISTIAN MISSION EFFORTS

If it is so (and I believe that it is) that all people and cultures can have some knowledge of God and can be pleasing to God without any special revelation, whether Jewish or Christian, then why do we need Christian mission efforts? Because, very simply, the world is full of sin-filled rebels against God and broken failures before God. Here the apostle Paul comes to our aid once again: "though they knew God, they did not honor him as God or give thanks to him, but they became futile in their thinking, and their senseless minds were darkened" (Rom 1:21).

So, in our mission efforts we share the good news of Jesus as Savior, Teacher, Lord, and Friend to all people freely, without proselytizing them for our culture, even our religious culture, where it is not essential as an expression of love of God and neighbor.

THE HEAVENLY TREASURE AND THE EARTHEN VESSEL

Now, in our sharing this good news of life with Jesus in the kingdom of God it is of utmost importance that we distinguish the heavenly treasure from the earthen vessel in which we carry it. Paul declared, "We have this treasure in earthen vessels" (2 Cor 4:7 NASB1995). The heavenly treasure, as Paul makes clear, is "the knowledge of the glory of God in the face of Jesus Christ" (2 Cor 4:6). The earthen vessel is the human body and the many cultural forms we use to enshroud the treasure. There is one heavenly treasure . . . there are many earthen vessels. What we are to pass on to people is the heavenly treasure, not the earthen vessels.

The number and variety of earthen vessels is as infinite as human personality: from high church to low church, from the quiet and introverted to the expressive and extroverted, from the articulate and rational to the emotive and compassionate. And so much more.

I suppose, if we worked really hard, we could discover certain values of one vessel over against another . . . but I doubt that it would be worth much. These are all *earthen* vessels.

We simply do not redeem people by imposing *our* earthen vessel on others. No, we allow every people group to discover their own earthen vessel in which they are enabled to enshroud the heavenly treasure. If we impose our earthen vessel on others, as Jesus tells us, it will only end up making the new convert "twice as much a child of hell as yourselves" (Mt 23:15).

Our task—our only task—is to share the good news of Jesus as the Lover of our souls and the Deliverer of sin-plagued human beings and allow the Holy Spirit to draw people into the kingdom of God based on this message alone.

Well, this is my take. I could be wrong, of course, and would be glad for any who have a concern to enlighten me further on this matter. Now back to humility.

(((((FOURTH WEEK)))))

An Exceptional Humility

Regarding humility Ohiyesa writes, "We first Americans mingle with our pride an exceptional humility. Spiritual arrogance is foreign to our nature and teaching. We never claimed that the power of articulate speech is proof of superiority over 'dumb creation'; on the other hand, it is to us a perilous gift."

An interesting combination this mingling "with our pride an exceptional humility." Normally we think of pride as the enemy of humility. Here Ohiyesa is speaking of pride in a positive light . . . a right kind of pride that sits comfortably with humility of spirit. I will allow this matter to stew for a while.

The Unseen and the Eternal

Here is a lovely sample of Ohiyesa's writings on prayer:

> Prayer—the daily recognition of the Unseen and the Eternal—is our one inevitable duty. . . . We wake at daybreak, put on our moccasins and step down to the water's edge. Here we throw handfuls of clear, cold water into our face, or plunge in bodily.
>
> After the bath, we stand erect before the advancing dawn, facing the sun as it dances upon the horizon, and offer our unspoken prayer. Our mate may proceed or follow us in our devotions, but never accompanies us. Each soul must meet the morning sun, the new sweet earth, and the Great Silence alone.

It intrigues me that he insists on this being a solitary experience. I have found it to be so, perhaps because personal prayer and devotion is so deeply individualized. Also, I note that this prayer is unspoken . . . personalized to the nth degree. It is quite different from say the singing of hymns that is meant to be a corporate experience.

DISPLAY AND SELF-AGGRANDIZEMENT

Ohiyesa had a keen eye to the hypocrisy of many of the Christians he met: "There was undoubtedly much in primitive Christianity to appeal to the Indians, and Jesus' hard sayings to the rich and about the rich were entirely comprehensible to us. Yet the religion that we heard preached in churches and saw practiced by congregations, with its element of display and self-aggrandizement, its active proselytism, and its open contempt of all religions but its own, was for a long time extremely repellent."

Well, it should be repellent . . . even repulsive. I also note that he is immediately sensitive to the display of self-aggrandizement in the Christians he meets. (Oh my. I can hardly spell "self-aggrandizement," and here Ohiyesa—whose primary language is Lakota—uses it so expertly. Wow!) I wonder what he would think of the internet and TV preachers of our day. Today it seems that self-aggrandizement has jumped to the tenth power!

WOULD THAT ALL THE LORD'S PEOPLE WERE PROPHETS

Today I am meditating on Moses the man. Scripture says of him, "Now the man Moses was very humble, more so than anyone else on the face of the earth" (Num 12:3). There is one story, found in Numbers 11, that for me wonderfully illustrates this description of Moses.

It occurs during an especially trying time for Moses . . . no longer in Egypt but not yet in the Promised Land. The people are complaining bitterly and Moses is dead-dog weary from his leadership responsibilities, so much so that he wishes to die.

The Lord responds by promising to share some of the burden Moses is carrying with seventy of the elders of Israel. So, God instructs Moses to bring the seventy to the tent of meeting, and once gathered God will take some of the "spirit" that is on Moses and place it on the seventy and "they shall bear the burden of the people along with you so that you will not bear it all by yourself." Moses does as he is instructed.

The seventy gather . . . well, not exactly . . . sixty-eight of the seventy gather. Two of the seventy, Eldad and Medad by name, miss the meeting. Anyway, the Lord does indeed take some of the spirit that is on Moses and place it on the seventy "and when the spirit rested upon them, they prophesied." Wow—that must have been a lively group experience!

Now, here is the kicker in the story. Eldad and Medad are down in the camp with the people "and the spirit rested on them" and they also prophesied. Well, when word of this gets back to everyone at the tent of meeting, Joshua demands that Moses at once stop Eldad and Medad, who are down in the camp, from prophesying.

In Moses' response to Joshua we are able to get a glimpse into the heart of Moses. We see a heart that has been humbled before God and that walks in great humility of spirit. Moses replies, "Are you jealous for my sake? Would that all the Lord's people were prophets, and that the Lord would put his spirit on them!"

Oh, I pray for this response of Moses in the heart and mind of every leader today, "Would that all the Lord's people were prophets, and that the Lord would put his spirit on them!" Yes, indeed.

A GENUINELY REGAL WALK

Early this morning I saw a fox. I was having morning coffee out on our back deck . . . and there he was. He had quietly stepped out from the base of a nearby pine. I wouldn't have noticed him at all except that when he stepped from around the tree the morning sun shone directly on his face. We looked straight at each other, me and the fox, for a long moment and then he turned and walked away. A genuinely regal walk. The sun caught his bushy red tail and it gave the impression of a goodbye wave. Is this the "mingling with our pride an exceptional humility" that Ohiyesa speaks of? I wonder.

Well, meeting the fox in the morning sunlight was an unexpected moment. It made my day.

The Moon When the Wind Shakes Off the Leaves

OCTOBER 8–NOVEMBER 4

For thus says the high and lofty one
who inhabits eternity, whose name is Holy:
I dwell in the high and holy place,
and also with those who are contrite and humble in spirit,
to revive the spirit of the humble,
and to revive the heart of the contrite.

YAHWEH (ISAIAH 57:15)

Humility and fear of God surpass all other virtues.

ABBA JOHN THE DWARF

(((((FIRST WEEK)))))

THIS PERSISTENT INTEGRITY

The tenth Lakota virtue is *Cantewasake,* "fortitude." It is said of this virtue, "After learning patience and inner endurance one gains the strength necessary to have fortitude. Emotional stability, being alert, and having determination can help in having this persistent integrity. This is not an inflexible force. It is a quiet, gentle voice of a Grandmother with deep faith, trust, and understanding."

"Persistent integrity" . . . feels like a good way of thinking about fortitude. Then, it helps if we are able to tie this to the "quiet, gentle voice of a Grandmother" who keeps urging us to stick with it. So, this month I will endeavor to keep this persistent integrity in my mind.

This brings to my mind the words of James about trials producing endurance: "My brothers and sisters, whenever you face trials of any kind, consider it nothing but joy, because you know that the testing of your faith produces endurance; and let endurance have its full effect, so that you may be mature and complete, lacking in nothing" (Jas 1:2-4). Endurance . . . fortitude . . . leading to humility of heart.

I would like to think about the ways humility and fortitude complement each other. I will live with this for the next few days and see if anything emerges.

The Birth of Obedience in the Heart

This morning I wake up to the first snow of the season. Only three or four inches but it's enough to flock the woods out my study window. Wonder-filled! It will melt soon with our warm weather but still . . . lovely, lovely, lovely.

No fire today since over the summer I have accumulated a generous stack of books and papers in front of the fireplace. Still, I sit in my rocking chair for some moments watching the snow come down gently. I punch up a Christmas CD and began cleaning the books and papers away from the fireplace so that next time I will be ready for a roaring blaze.

As I work away I come across these words from Thomas Kelly of *Testament of Devotion* fame, "humility and holiness are twins in the astonishing birth of obedience in the heart." Is he saying that humility of heart and purity of life work together to produce obedience toward God? I think so. I will see what I can do to put this into practice and see what I learn.

TEXTURE AND FEELING TONES

A morning hike in a nearby canyon is utterly refreshing. The landscape has turned rust-colored brown almost overnight. All the plant life is preparing for the winter season that is soon to come. But today the sun warms me. Along the trail I can see little patches of snow that have effectively hid from the sun.

Human hikers (except for me) are nonexistent, due I imagine to the snow of the other day. Hence, I am able to hike in complete silence. I hear only the twitter of the rosy finches in the trees and the gurgle of the creek below. The silence does me good. The "brown" of plant and rock draw me down toward the earth. There is a kind of humility in my getting down close to the earth. Humility . . . *humus*. Hiking quietly, without a word. No one knows of my presence, except the mule deer and black squirrels . . . and they could not seem to care less.

These times provide texture and feeling tones to the word *humility*.

(((((SECOND WEEK)))))

THE SMALL CORNERS OF LIFE

Early this morning I sense a divine nudge to learn about humility in the "small corners" of life. Lord, show me ways to express a humble spirit in these small corners.

The first order of the day is to take Carolynn to a medical appointment. Once there I wait . . . and I wait . . . and I wait. It is not unusual this waiting, but I am wondering if this is one way I am to learn humility today. Just wondering.

Then we decide we have time for me to get my flu shot for the season. So, off we go to my pharmacy. The lady who attends to us has difficulty with the computer system. Again, waiting. I sense her frustration and pray for her to find a way through the computer maze. Today, it is not to be. She finally gives up and asks me to come back another day. Okay.

Off we go to Carolynn's pharmacy to see if we might have better success. Indeed, we do. She has no problem with the computer . . . but the interruptions in her labors are maddening. I wait . . . and wait . . . and wait again. I muse that by learning a "patient waiting" I bring a humble spirit into my soul. On the other hand, a waiting that is filled with anxiety or anger thwarts humility of soul. So, I seek to orient myself to a "patient waiting." The pharmacist says it will be twenty minutes. Well, twenty minutes turns into thirty and thirty turns into forty. Perhaps more. I try not to check my watch.

At last we are rewarded and I receive my shot, thankful for the good care of the pharmacist. And everything is done in time to get Carolynn home so she can get to an afternoon appointment in time. So far so good.

I'm free now and I decide to go to the rec center for my exercise for the day. I make appropriate preparations and I am off. However, I forgot that this is late Friday afternoon and the freeway ten miles away has major construction delays and so traffic is diverted to our country roadway. I am five miles away from the roadway, and when I get to it I find traffic backed up for several miles behind the single light at our little intersection. I take one look at the long line of cars and decide I have learned enough about "humility-that-comes-through-waiting" for one day. I turn around and drive home. I get my exercise by using the treadmill downstairs. I'm glad for what I have learned and humbled by the experience.

TENDING THE FIRE OF MY SOUL

A wonderful snow of perhaps twelve inches over two days has turned our home into a winter wonderland. I need to clear off the driveway three different times, but once that is accomplished I can enjoy our quiet woods . . . the woods are always especially quiet after a good snow.

Most of all I am ready for a good, steady fire down in my study. The wood and the flames are good companions. In the late afternoon I think back to when I was a child of eight. We had wintered at an uncle's cabin deep in the Rocky Mountains. I slept in front of the generous fireplace. As this was our only heat source through the night, we needed to keep it burning. In time I became the person who tended the fire through the night. Tonight I am reminded that I need to be constantly tending the fire of my soul.

THE VOICE OF THE TRUE SHEPHERD

Today I go back to an old friend, John Woolman, and his famous journal. I am considering a passage where he is dealing with materialism and his relationship to this thorny subject. He brings up humility amid a discussion of simplicity of life: "I saw that an humble man, with the blessing of the Lord, might live on a little, and that where the heart was set on greatness, success in business did not satisfy the craving; but that commonly with an increase of wealth the desire of wealth increased. There was a care on my mind so to pass my time that nothing might hinder me from the most steady attention to the voice of the true Shepherd."

For Woolman the most important thing is a "steady attention to the voice of the true Shepherd." May this become true for me more and more . . . as I am ready and able to receive it.

(((((THIRD WEEK)))))

THE WISE APOSTLE PAUL

I am seeking to settle into the writings of the wise apostle Paul and especially his words on humility. They read like a rat-a-tat-tat of concern for the spirit of humility.

- Romans 12:10—"Outdo one another in showing honor."

- Romans 12:16—"Do not be haughty, but associate with the lowly."

- Galatians 5:13—"For you were called to freedom, brothers and sisters; only do not use your freedom as an opportunity for self-indulgence, but through love become slaves to one another."

- Ephesians 4:1-2—"Lead a life worthy of the calling to which you have been called, with all humility and gentleness, with patience, bearing with one another in love."

- Ephesians 5:21—"Be subject to one another out of reverence for Christ."

- Philippians 2:3—"Do nothing from selfish ambition or conceit, but in humility regard others as better than yourselves."

- Philippians 2:5-8—"Let the same mind be in you that was in Christ Jesus. . . . He humbled himself and became obedient to the point of death—even death on a cross."

- Colossians 3:12—"Clothe yourselves with compassion, kindness, humility, meekness, and patience."

And to top it all off we have Paul's magnificent essay on *agape* love in 1 Corinthians 13. Here we find humility hidden inside *agape* as an essential ingredient: "Love is patient; love is kind; love is not envious or boastful or arrogant or rude. It does not insist on its own way; it is not irritable or resentful; it does not rejoice in wrongdoing, but rejoices in the truth. It bears all things, believes all things, hopes all things, endures all things."

How is it that Paul learned the spirit of humility so deeply in his soul? Did he learn lessons in humility as he stood watching Stephen's death? The many disciples of Jesus that Paul persecuted surely taught him about a life of humble service. I rather imagine that his dramatic encounter with the risen Christ (strong enough to knock him off his donkey and blind him for a time) and his conversion experience with Ananias who addressed him as "brother Saul" taught him the ABCs of humility. Even more important were his three years in the deserts of Arabia, where I rather imagine he was constantly learning directly from his divine Teacher Jesus. Most certainly Paul learned well what a life of humility in the interior chambers of the heart looks like. Oh, may I too learn the supreme value of humility of heart.

((((FOURTH WEEK))))

THE MOST GRACIOUS ECUMENICAL SPIRIT

Andrew Murray was a Scottish preacher and pastor of the nineteenth century. Virtually all of his ministry years were spent in South Africa. We know him today because of his many books of Christian devotion, perhaps the most well-known being *With Christ in the School of Prayer*. My early training in the life of devotion came to a large extent from Andrew Murray's writings.

I single him out here because of a slender volume (just over a hundred pages) he wrote with the simple title *Humility*. Indeed, the title is so unassuming that more recent editions of the book have sought to embellish it a bit with subtitles like *True Greatness* or *The Beauty of Holiness* or *The Journey Toward Holiness*. These are justified only because Murray devotes chapter seven to humility in relationship to holiness, especially the Keswick holiness movement in his day, sometimes called the Higher Life movement. But the central focus of Murray's book is the Christian virtue of humility.

I appreciate many things about this small book. One emphasis of Murray's we can easily miss is the ease with which he uses epigraphs from Roman Catholic writers of devotion to begin many chapters. Remember, in the nineteenth century the Dutch Reformed Church in which Murray was ordained was not especially warm toward the Church of Rome . . . to put it mildly. Add to this that Murray's mother was a descendent of the French Huguenots who had been so severely persecuted by Rome, almost to extinction. Yet, in this small book I find Andrew Murray showing the most gracious ecumenical spirit, drawing from a breadth of sources:

- Thomas Aquinas—"If you are looking for an example of humility, look at the cross."
- Thomas à Kempis—"The more humble a man is in himself, the more obedient toward God, the wiser will he be in all things, and the more shall his soul be at peace."
- Bernard of Clairvaux—"It is no great thing to be humble when you are brought low; but to be humble when you are praised is a great and rare achievement."
- Augustine of Hippo—"Should you ask me: What is the first thing in religion? I should reply: the first, second, and third thing herein is humility."

Lovely. I like the quotations and, even more, I like that Murray used them.

The Root of All

Andrew Murray himself says: "Humility is the only soil in which virtue takes root; a lack of humility is the explanation of every defect and failure. Humility is not so much a virtue along with the others, but is the root of all."

Again, "The call to humility has been too little regarded in the church because its true nature and importance have been too little apprehended."

Then Murray shares with us his own lack and learning about humility: "I had long known the Lord without realizing that meekness and lowliness of heart are to be the distinguishing feature of the disciple, just as they were of the Master."

Finally, Murray deals with pride, which he considers the crux of our problem:

> Let us at the very outset . . . admit that there is nothing so natural to man, nothing so insidious and hidden from our sight, nothing so difficult and dangerous as pride. And acknowledge that nothing but a very determined and persevering waiting on God will reveal how lacking we are in the grace of humility and how powerless we are to obtain what we seek. We must study the character of Christ until our souls are filled with the love and admiration of His lowliness.

Satan at the Headwaters of Pride

Murray sees pride as the great enemy of humility. And he stresses repeatedly that Satan is at the headwaters of pride. In one significant passage Murray speaks of "the pride Satan breathed into humankind."

The epigraph to lead off chapter eight ("Humility and Sin") contains a quote from Jonathan Edwards that I had never read before: "Nothing sets a person so much out of the devil's reach as humility."

The theme of pride originating in Satan is sprinkled throughout *Humility*. It is probably not the way we would write about the issue today, but for this very reason it has unusual punch. It underscores for me the need to be aware that the Enemy of our soul uses pride as his chief weapon. So, all the more need for me to cultivate humility of heart.

THE BEST OF ALL THE GRACES

On this subject Murray was keenly aware of the failure of the church in his day: "It seems that the church has failed to teach its people the importance of humility—that it is the first of the virtues, the best of all the graces and powers of the Spirit."

If Murray's words are an accurate description of the church in the nineteenth century . . . how much truer of us today. Precious little in today's culture encourages humility of heart. Pastors find it exceedingly difficult to address the subject in their preaching. And the average Christian has so few living examples of how to live quietly and humbly.

O Lord, forgive us for our lack. Teach us a good way forward.

EVERY KIND AND FORM AND DEGREE OF PRIDE

Murray concludes his slender book with an experimental prayer for humility.

> I will here give you an infallible touchstone that will test all to the truth: retire from the world and all conversation for one month. Neither write, nor read, nor debate anything with yourself; stop all the former workings of your heart and mind, and with all the strength of your heart stand as continually as you can in the following form of prayer to God. Offer it

frequently on your knees; but whether sitting, walking, or standing, be always inwardly longing and earnestly praying this one prayer to God: that of His great goodness He would make known to you, and take from your heart every kind and form and degree of pride, . . . and that He would awaken in you the deepest depth and truth of that humility which can make you capable of His light and Holy Spirit.

I am not sure I could manage Murray's one-month time frame . . . but his prayer for humility most certainly speaks to my condition. O Lord, God of all mercy, take from my heart every kind and form and degree of pride. Awaken in me the deepest depth and truth of that humility which can make me capable of your light and Holy Spirit. Amen.

The Moon of the Rutting Deer

NOVEMBER 5–DECEMBER 3

"God opposes the proud, but gives grace to the humble." Submit
yourselves therefore to God. Resist the devil, and he will flee from
you. Draw near to God, and he will draw near to you. Cleanse your
hands, you sinners, and purify your hearts, you double-minded. . . .
Humble yourselves before the Lord, and he will exalt you.

JAMES 4:6-10

If you look for merciful love you will find it among the humble
ones. Humility is the place where justice resides.

APHRAHAT THE PERSIAN SAGE

(((((FIRST WEEK)))))

A TIMELESS VIRTUE

The eleventh Lakota virtue is *Canteyuke,* "generosity." Here is a description: "'To have a heart' is the literal translation of this Lakota word which is a timeless virtue residing in the heart. True generosity has always been encouraged and exemplified in Lakota society while accumulating material possessions was greatly discouraged. As our Earth Mother gives everything, we should in turn do the same. True generosity embodies love and the understanding of impermanence."

Generosity meaning, "to have a heart." I like that very much . . . I need that very much. Oh how I need heart today; a heart for the outcast, a heart for the lonely, a heart for the down and out, a heart for the up and in. Lord, increase my heart toward my neighbor . . . my *neigh-bor*, the person who is near me.

THE HAPPINESS OF HUMILITY

This afternoon I receive a note from Brian, who knows about both my humility project and my keen appreciation for John Woolman: "Your stories about Woolman prompted me to dig back into his Journal. What a remarkable man. This morning I read this: 'But through the revelation of Jesus Christ, I had seen the happiness of humility, and there was an earnest desire in me to enter deep into it; and at times this desire arose to a degree of fervent supplication, wherein my soul was so environed with heavenly light and consolation that things were made easy to me which had been otherwise.'"

I thought I had scoured through Woolman's journal writings from top to bottom, but this passage comes to me as if brand new. O how I would love to experience more fully "the happiness of humility." And O how I wish for my soul to be "environed with heavenly light."

A NEW HISTORY OF INDIGENOUS POWER

In these journal notes I have tended to focus on Lakota life experiences in the Black Hills and their efforts to retain this region. Of course, there is far more to their story, and an excellent source for learning the larger story is a rather hefty book by Pekka Hämäläinen titled *Lakota America: A New History of Indigenous Power*.

Hämäläinen seeks to recover "the untold story of the Lakotas from the sixteenth into the twenty-first century and it also recovers the story of the North American interior, the immense swath of land stretching from the Great Lakes to the Rocky Mountains and from the Canadian Shield to the edges of the American South."

In the mid-seventeenth century the Lakotas had been an obscure tribe of hunters and gatherers centered mainly in the Great Lakes region. Even though they were lacking metal weapons or political clout they began to establish what Hämäläinen describes as

> the most improbable expansion in American history. Lakotas left their ancient homelands and reinvented themselves as horse people in the continental grasslands that stretched seemingly forever into the horizon. This was the genesis of what I call Lakota America, an expansive, constantly transmuting Indigenous regime that pulled numerous groups into its orbit. . . . Another century later they were the most powerful Indigenous nation in the Americas, controlling a massive domain stretching across the northern Great Plains into the Rocky Mountains and Canada.

It seems to me that the Lakota found a way to wield power that affirmed their right to protect their culture and land but did not force domination and control on other people groups. Indeed, they seem to have been masters at building their strengths from within, rather than from seizing the resources of other cultures to claim as theirs alone. A history lesson for our day, to be sure.

(((((SECOND WEEK)))))

A Prayer at Coffee Time

In the middle of the first moon of my little experiment into humility (The Hard Moon) I sought divine guidance for a prayer that might carry me through the entire year. After a few days the prayer that emerged was a simple four-part petition:

Lord Jesus, I invite you to . . .
Purify my heart,
Renew my mind,
Sanctify my imagination, and
Enlarge my soul.
Amen.

Often I pray in this way over a morning cup of coffee. At times I may sense a divine invitation to linger over one particular area . . . heart, mind, imagination, soul. Instruction or guidance may be given, and, perhaps, confession from me. Most of all there is the stillness of a familiar friendship. I seek to keep praying in this way even when my heart seems to wander far from the purity I seek. My little prayer sometimes follows me throughout the day . . . *purify* . . . *renew* . . . *sanctify* . . . *enlarge*.

I am now twelve moons (eleven months) into this simple experiment in prayer, and one change I am noticing is a gentle shifting in my desires. Some desires are quietly dropping away and others are rising up. For example, ever so slowly I feel myself drawn more deeply into experiencing the life-giving words of Frederick W. Faber:

Only to sit and think of God,
Oh what a joy it is!
To think the thought, to breathe the Name
Earth has no higher bliss.

I am sure I have much more to learn. But I thank God for the quiet shifts in desire I am detecting already. Step by step!

A Tender Heart and a Humble Mind

This afternoon I find myself meditating on the relationship between humility and grace. The words of James 4:6 comes to mind, "God opposes the proud, but gives grace to the humble." The same words are echoed in 1 Peter 5:5, "God opposes the proud, but gives grace to the humble."

In 2 Peter 3:18 we are urged to "grow in the grace and knowledge of our Lord and Savior Jesus Christ." We, it seems, can *grow* in grace. Then, in 1 Peter 3:8 we are instructed to "have unity of spirit, sympathy, love for one another, a tender heart, and a humble mind."

So, I think it is safe to say that humility opens the door for receiving grace from God. And, in turn, grace is multiplied to us as we cultivate humility of heart and mind. Grace upon grace.

O Lord, root out the arrogance and pride that seeks to establish residence in me. Instead, instill deep within "a tender heart and a humble mind." Amen.

The Complete Anti-God State of Mind

I have not thought deeply enough about *pride* as the most vicious enemy of humility. Lewis in his famous chapter "The Great Sin" writes, "The essential vice, the utmost evil, is Pride. Unchastity, anger, greed, drunkenness, and all that, are mere fleabites in comparison: it was through Pride that the devil became the devil: Pride leads to every other vice: it is the complete anti-God state of mind."

O Lord, teach me the horridness, the awfulness of pride. Let this reality sink deep down into my consciousness. Cause my spirit to react instinctively to the very presence of pride and to flee from it. Purify my heart so utterly that no hint of pride is able to reside inside. This I pray in the strong name of Jesus. Amen.

Pride Slips in Unawares

This morning Nate and I took a hike in the backside of the canyon. We took the Old Homestead loop that normally is an hour and a half hike . . . though nowadays I find the time creeping up toward two hours. Ordinarily, we would hike the loop clockwise, but today we decided to go counterclockwise, which makes staying on the main trail a little trickier.

About half an hour in we came upon a large flock of wild turkeys scratching and pecking among the dense scrub oak. We watched for a time while I counted twenty-nine, maybe thirty turkeys. They paid no attention to us and continued their foraging for food. Ten minutes further on we encountered another flock of what appeared to be an equal number . . . I think, I couldn't get a good count. These two flocks are by far the largest number of wild turkeys I have ever seen in one place. Astonishing!

We hiked on. Several times we would come to a fork in the trail and Nate would wait for me to nod left or right. Nate has been on this trail before but never in reverse . . . and I have hiked it so many times that I began imagining I could probably hike it with my eyes closed. I felt rather pleased with the thought. This went on until near the end of our hike we came to a final fork in the trail and I said casually, "Right." Within twenty paces I knew we had taken the wrong trail. Humbled and well chastised, I had us backtrack to the main trail.

Astonishing how quickly and quietly pride slips in unawares.

(((((THIRD WEEK)))))

Glorying in Undeserved Honors

I have just happened on a new resource for my thinking about humility: *Spiritual Practices of Jesus: Learning Simplicity, Humility and*

Prayer with Luke's Earliest Readers by Catherine J. Wright. Right now I am only reading what I can find on the internet so I have yet to read the book. She has three chapters devoted to humility: (1) Humility in the Gospel Narrative, (2) Humility Through First-Century Eyes, and (3) Learning Humility with the Church.

I'm eager to get the whole book . . . but I captured a nice statement on humility through the material I was able to access: "Humility, rooted in an accurate self-assessment, rejects arrogant pride, which is seen in a desire to gain or maintain status, glorying in undeserved honors, and self-praise."

I am especially taken with the phrase "glorying in undeserved honors." Oh my, this is where I stand nowadays. People say such nice things . . . some are accurate but others are way over the top. I shudder sometimes at the "undeserved" accolades well-meaning folk send my way. Lord, teach me to discern the "accurate" from the "undeserved" and allow the undeserved to simply slip away. Amen.

I Remember with Gratitude

In the United States today is Thanksgiving Day, one holiday that is indeed worth remembering . . . minus the mythical embellishments about Indians and pilgrims. So, today I remember with gratitude the lives of Lawrence ("Gunner") and Helen Payne. Our paths crossed numerous times over the years. The first was before I had even met Gunner and Helen when a dozen of us gathered in retreat at their mountain cabin at Lake Arrowhead to dream and plan a summer mission trip to Kotzebue, Alaska, ostensibly to build the first high school above the Arctic Circle. Gathering at the Payne cabin took me back to my childhood time wintering at a cabin in the Rocky Mountains, and the planning did indeed lead to a trip of a lifetime living and working among the Inupiaq Eskimo people.

Gunner and Helen were almost legendary among Quakers in California, certainly because of their loving and humble service, but also because of a terrible tragedy that occurred in their family. Ruby Ann, their teenage daughter, had gone to babysit the three children of a neighboring farmer. Unexpectedly, William Rupp, the farm handyman, appeared at the back door. He sent the children off on an errand. While they were away, he abused and brutally murdered Ruby Ann and then fled into the nearby hills.

When the murder was discovered a group of men from town gathered to hunt down Rupp, enraged and seeking vengeance. On that horrific day a close friend of Gunner made the astonishing statement that the safest place that William Rupp could have been found that night was not up in the hills of Yorba Linda but with Ruby Ann's parents, Gunner and Helen Payne.

William Rupp was caught, charged with first-degree murder, and sentenced to die in the gas chamber. For the six years before Rupp's execution, Gunner was a regular visitor. He extended to William the completely undeserved gift of forgiveness and, in God's time and in God's way, led him to a saving relationship with Jesus.

I met Gunner through my warm friendship with his and Helen's son, Preston. (Sadly, the family suffered even more tragedy—as a young man Preston was in a terrible auto accident, which ever after damaged his speech and mobile abilities.) It was Gunner, a laborer by trade and a father who had suffered so much, who taught me to appreciate the writings of François Fénelon. Whenever we met he would ask enthusiastically, "Richard, have you read Fénelon's *Christian Perfection*?" Well, I had tried, after a manner of speaking . . . but I always tried by speed reading it, and one simply does not speed read Fénelon, and so I would give up. But Gunner would stay with me urging me repeatedly to give Fénelon another try. Finally, with great patience, Gunner taught me to read ever so slowly . . .

to read with the heart. I will always thank Gunner Payne for that lesson.

I today remember the loving, humble lives of Gunner and Helen Payne.

THE MORE WE LOVE PURELY

Remembering Gunner causes me over morning coffee to open Fénelon's *Christian Perfection*. Because of my daily focus on humility these words jump out at me, "All the saints are convinced that sincere humility is the foundation of all virtues. This is because humility is the daughter of pure charity, and humility is nothing else but truth. . . . Jesus Christ said that we must be meek and humble of heart. Meekness is the daughter of humility, as anger is the daughter of pride. Only Jesus Christ can give that true humility of heart which comes from him. . . . He, who does not seek his own interest, but the interest of God alone in time and for eternity, is humble. The more we love purely, the more perfect is our humility."

My, how Fénelon teaches me . . . if I can be slow enough and patient enough to learn.

DEVASTATION AND DESPAIR

Today is the beginning of Advent in the Christian calendar. This season, which lasts about a month, is designed to help me wait expectantly for the coming of the babe of Bethlehem . . . "born a child and yet a King," to borrow words from Charles Wesley's wonderful Advent hymn.

However, I am not ready for the Advent season . . . not yet. My mind is fixated on one month ahead . . . December 29, to be exact. This will be the 130th anniversary of the grisly massacre of Lakota men, women, and children at Wounded Knee, December 29, 1890.

Here is a little of what led up to what Black Elk described as "the butchering at Wounded Knee." In 1887 Congress passed the Dawes Severalty Act and the Sioux Agreement, which called for the breakup of the Great Sioux Reservation into smaller, more manageable units. As a result the Great Sioux Reservation was carved up into five isolated islands of controllable size. The remaining lands (half of the original reservation) were ceded to white settlers.

Then came the severe winter of 1889–1890, and Lakota families suffered extensive crop failures. Add to this an outbreak of whooping cough and influenza, which spread like wildfire among the people, with a particularly heavy toll falling on the children.

In the midst of all this devastation and despair came a Paiute "holy man and prophet" by the name of Wovoka. He shared with the destitute Lakota a prophetic message of hope, rebirth, and deliverance. His vision promised the resurrection of the Lakota who had died, the return of *tatanka*, and the restoring of the old indigenous world. This prophetic vision of a restored earth and a better world gripped the Lakota people.

To bring about this prophetic vision of resurrected kin, of restored bison, and of a world without disease, the Lakota began dancing and singing in what has come to be known as "the Ghost Dance." Some Lakota wore special dresses and shirts which were supposed to protect them against bullets.

Army officers and Indian agents were alarmed at this frenetic activity. At Pine Ridge a new agent wired Washington asking for troops because the "Indians are dancing in the snow & are wild & crazy." President Benjamin Harrison authorized an armed response, sending six to seven thousand soldiers to Lakota country concerned that, in the words of General Nelson A. Miles, "the most serious Indian war in history was at hand." An effort to arrest Lakota leader Chief Sitting Bull went terribly wrong. Sitting Bull was shot, first in the back and then in the head, dying in front of his log cabin.

The followers of Sitting Bull sought refuge in the camp of Chief Spotted Elk. Army officers considered Spotted Elk to be Sitting Bull's successor and a key hostile. Spotted Elk himself was seriously ill with pneumonia and was on his way to Pine Ridge to find a place to rest. General Miles did not allow this and instead ordered Spotted Elk and his followers to be disarmed and detained.

General Miles assigned the Seventh Cavalry under the command of Colonel James W. Forsyth to escort Spotted Elk and his followers to the Wounded Knee Creek. Once at Wounded Knee Colonel Forsyth ordered the Lakota rounded up for the night and had four Hotchkiss cannons placed on a hill overlooking their camp.

The next morning Colonel Forsyth ordered that all weapons be removed from the Lakota. One Lakota man, Yellow Bird, resisted, asking to be paid for his gun. In the ensuing struggle with a military officer the gun went off, killing the officer . . . this was all it took for the Seventh Cavalry to begin firing, and the four cannons sent deadly shells raining down on the camp. Most of the men were killed almost instantly and the women and children took shelter in a ravine behind the camp. Whatever resistance there was ended in minutes, but the killing continued for over half an hour, followed by point-blank executions. Nearly three hundred Lakotas were killed that day at Wounded Knee, over half of them women and children.

General Miles was highly critical of the command of Colonel Forsyth and would later describe Wounded Knee as "the most abominable criminal military blunder and a horrible massacre of women and children."

Most who know of this horrific event have learned about it from Dee Brown's fine book, *Bury My Heart at Wounded Knee,* penned in 1970. It covers the years from 1860 with the Long Walk of the Navajos to 1890 with the massacre at Wounded Knee.

THE NATION'S HOOP IS BROKEN

My most helpful source about Wounded Knee is the 1932 book *Black Elk Speaks,* for Black Elk was a witness to the horrendous events. In 1890 Black Elk was a young man of twenty-seven and was in the Pine Ridge area at the time. He heard the terrible sound of "wagon guns" (cannons) going off. He describes what happens next:

> I saddled up my buckskin and put on my sacred shirt. It was one I had made to be worn by no one but myself. . . . I painted my face all red, and in my hair I put one eagle feather for the One Above. It did not take me long to get ready, for I could still hear the shooting over there. I started out alone on the old road that ran across the hills to Wounded Knee. I had no gun. I carried only the sacred bow of the west that I had seen in my great vision.

Black Elk rode at top speed, and then, "the shooting was getting louder. A horseback from over there came galloping very fast toward us, and he said: 'Hey-hey-hey! They have murdered them!' Then he whipped his horse and rode away faster toward Pine Ridge."

Black Elk rode on to the top of the ridge where he could look down into Wounded Knee; "wagon guns were still going off over there on the little hill, and they were going off again where they hit along the gulch. There was much shooting down yonder, and there were many cries. . . . Cavalrymen were riding along the gulch and shooting into it where the women and children were running away and trying to hide in the gullies and the stunted pines."

Black Elk himself charged at the soldiers holding his sacred bow out toward them in his right hand. They shot at him and he could hear the bullets zinging past but none hit him. Other soldiers across the gulch began shooting at him too, but he was not hurt.

Black Elk continues,

> By now many other Lakotas, who had heard the shooting, were coming up from Pine Ridge. . . . We followed down along the dry gulch, and what we saw was terrible. Dead and wounded women and children and little babies were scattered all along there where they had been trying to run away. The soldiers had followed along the gulch, as they ran, and murdered them in there. Sometimes they were in heaps because they had huddled together, and some were scattered all along. Sometimes bunches of them had been killed and torn to pieces where the wagon guns hit them. I saw a little baby trying to suck its mother, but she was bloody and dead.

As Black Elk concludes his heartbreaking description he adds, "When I saw this I wished that I had died too."

The massacre at Wounded Knee occurred on a bright winter day. By that evening a howling wind came up followed by a vicious blizzard. The bitter cold froze the bodies into grossly contorted shapes. Black Elk observes, "The snow drifted deep in the crooked gulch, and it was one long grave of butchered women and children and babies, who had never done any harm and were only trying to run away."

Black Elk concludes,

> And so it was all over. I did not know then how much was ended. When I look back now from this high hill of my old age, I can still see the butchered women and children lying heaped and scattered all along the crooked gulch as plain as when I saw them with eyes still young. And I can see that something else died there in the bloody mud, and was buried in the blizzard. A people's dream died there. It was a beautiful dream.

And I, to whom so great a vision was given in my youth,—you see me now a pitiful old man who has done nothing, for the nation's hoop is broken and scattered. There is no center any longer and the sacred tree is dead.

For Black Elk the tragedy of Wounded Knee meant the end of a culture and a way of life. This evening, in my feeble efforts to recount this enormous crucible of grief, my heart is saddened beyond the telling.

The Moon When the Deer Shed Their Antlers

DECEMBER 4–31

Create in me a clean heart, O God,
And put a new and right spirit within me.

DAVID (PSALM 51:10)

Just as one goes down into the bowels of the earth to find gold, so the
one who humbles himself with the gold of humility extracts all virtues.

EVAGRIUS OF PONTUS

(((((FIRST WEEK)))))

KNOWING THE DIFFERENCE BETWEEN
TRUTH AND ILLUSION

Finally, the twelfth and final of the Lakota virtues is *Woksape,*
"wisdom." This virtue is described like this:

> Only after one has learned about life and is able to act on all
> the other virtues, can one be considered wise. First we attain
> knowledge then we learn to apply that knowledge. Wisdom
> is acting on what you know. Our gift to life is wisdom as well
> as life's gift to us. It is knowing the difference between truth
> and illusion. One can have knowledge without wisdom but
> one cannot have wisdom without knowledge. Wisdom is a
> reward from life for persevering through all the virtues.

So, we now have all twelve of the Lakota virtues: humility, perseverance, respect, honor, love, sacrifice, truth, compassion, bravery, fortitude, generosity, and wisdom.

Over these past dozen "moons" I have come to appreciate these virtues a great deal and hope that more and more they will become a part of my daily living. I'm struck by how wonderful it is that wisdom concludes this list. Perhaps it is the culminating virtue, birthed in us as we give attention to all the others—a reward we receive, deepening our experience of continuing in the virtues. What a wonderful cycle of growth.

Preaching in Advent Was the Hardest

The Advent season is here. The two watchwords for this season are "expectant waiting" and "preparation" . . . first to celebrate the coming of the Christ child and second to anticipate Christ's glorious return. I'm not so sure about the "expectant waiting" part, but I think it will help me in "preparation" if I read and soak in a couple Advent sermons.

The first is by my closest friend in life William Luther Vaswig . . . Bill to me. For many years Bill pastored Lutheran churches and was an extraordinary preacher. Bill is gone now, but here are some words he penned in November/December of 2000:

> We are now approaching Christmas through the Advent season. Of all the preaching I've done, preaching in Advent was the hardest. It is a jarring experience for me still, to go to church during Advent. While Advent hasn't received a lot of attention . . . it should because during Advent there is the clearest clash between 'secular Christmas warmth and cheer' and the more sober and even austere Advent texts of the Sunday gospel readings of the church. The preacher is even tempted to lose the good news of Christ's coming again in

depression, frustration and even anger because Advent church music is not Christmas carols. People hear the Christmas carols being played at the mall. "On Jordan's Banks the Baptist's Cry" is not very Christmasy, but we sing it during Advent.

Bill's words speak to my condition right now. For the past weeks I have been immersing myself in the horrendous events of Wounded Knee, December 29, 1890. Earlier I offered the gist of that dark chapter in our history. So, my heart is not yet ready for the warmth of Christmas cheer. Leave it to a Lutheran pastor to remind me of the more somber preparation of which Advent speaks. Here are the lyrics of the hymn "On Jordan's Banks the Baptist's Cry" Bill mentioned.

On Jordan's bank the Baptist's cry
announces that the Lord is nigh.
Awake and harken, for he brings
glad tidings of the King of Kings!
Then cleansed be every life from sin:
make straight the way for God within,
and let us all our hearts prepare
for Christ to come and enter there.
We hail you as our Savior, Lord,
our refuge and our great reward.
Without your grace we waste away
like flowers that wither and decay.
Stretch forth your hand, our health restore,
and make us rise to fall no more.
O let your face upon us shine
and fill the world with love divine.
All praise to you, eternal Son,

whose advent has our freedom won,
whom with the Father we adore,
and Holy Spirit, evermore.

LET ME WALK IN BEAUTY

Today I came upon a Lakota prayer from the Aktá Lakota Museum and Cultural Center. Chief Yellow Lark has translated the prayer into English.

The Great Spirit Prayer

Oh, Great Spirit, whose voice I hear in the wind, whose
   breath gives life to all the world.
Hear me; I need your strength and wisdom.
Let me walk in beauty, and make my eyes ever behold the
   red and purple sunset.
Make my hands respect the things you have made and my
   ears sharp to hear your voice.
Make me wise so that I may understand the things you have
   taught my people.
Help me to remain calm and strong in the face of all that
   comes towards me.
Let me learn the lessons you have hidden in every leaf
   and rock.
Help me seek pure thoughts and act with the intention of
   helping others.
Help me find compassion without empathy
   overwhelming me.
I seek strength, not to be greater than my brother, but to
   fight my greatest enemy, Myself.

Make me always ready to come to you with clean hands and
    straight eyes.
So when life fades, as the fading sunset, my spirit may come
    to you without shame.

STILL WAITING

In the spring of 2018 there was a great gathering of Lakota people,
numbering in the thousands, at Fort Laramie National Historical Site
in Wyoming. Other Native nations attended as representatives. They
came to commemorate the 150th anniversary of the signing of the
1868 Treaty of Fort Laramie, which was violated when the Black Hills
Gold Rush made this five-thousand-mile, oval-shaped mountain
range suddenly valuable and Congress unilaterally annexed it in 1877.
Earlier this year I focused on this horrific act of greed in my Lenten
prayers during the Moon of the Sore Eyes. Now, in Advent, with the
terrible Wounded Knee anniversary approaching, I reflect on how
the Lakota Nation, having refused the financial compensation owed
to them under a 1980 Supreme Court case ruling, is still waiting for
the return of their tribal lands. The gathering in 2018 to honor the
spirit of the 1868 treaty signers has become a way for the Lakota
Nation to assert their self-determination.

Will they succeed? Is it possible for the Black Hills to be returned
to the Lakota Nation? A 2012 United Nations investigation advo-
cated exactly this. And in 2014 President Barack Obama visited the
Standing Rock Reservation and before eighteen hundred Native
Americans announced that nation-to-nation relationship should
be considered the rule. He then proposed that Congress could
return part of the Black Hills to the *Očhéthi Šakówiŋ*, or the Seven
Fires Council, the technical name for the Lakota Nation.

How feasible is this? I do not know. These questions are far
beyond my expertise to answer. However . . .

(((((THIRD WEEK)))))

A Hope and a Dream

The sun has begun to warm the day and so I decide on a long hike in the canyon. The winter sun feels good on my back. The hiking, however, is particularly slow because of the ice on the trail, especially in areas the sun's rays cannot reach. I have my trekking spikes on so it is safe . . . but I am slower than normal. As I plod along my brain is fixated on Wounded Knee and the Lakotas longing for their beloved *He Sapa*. What, if anything, can be done? A simple phrase begins bubbling up into my mind: "A hope and a dream." I *hope* for a day when *Mato Tipila* and Black Elk Peak and *Mato Paha* are once again reserved as sacred places for vision quests by the Lakota people. I *dream* of a day when reparations can occur that are just and right and good. I *hope* for a groundswell of sweeping calls for justice for the Lakota Nation. I *dream* of a day when Black Elk's vision of "the whole hoop of the world living together like one being" becomes a reality.

I know, I know. It is only a hope. It is only a dream. Still . . . may justice roll down like waters and righteousness like an ever-flowing stream.

The Lakotas Will Prevail

What about the future of the Lakota people? Can they survive the violence against them, the attacks on their sovereignty, the efforts to dismantle their rituals, the abuse and misuse of their history, the Dakota Access Pipeline oil leaks, and so much more. I wish I knew. I do not.

Rather, I will defer to and take heart in the concluding analysis of Pekka Hämäläinen in his monumental work, *Lakota America*: "Lakotas will endure because they are Iktómi's people, supple, accommodating, and absolutely certain of their essence even when becoming something new. There will be other governments, other regimes, and other epochs, but the Lakotas will prevail. They will always find a place in the world because they know how to be fully in it, adapting to its shape while remaking it, again and again, after their own image."

THE MAGNIFICAT

Another Advent sermon I have been eager to read is by Dietrich Bonhoeffer. Titled "My Spirit Rejoices," it centers on the Canticle of Mary found in Luke 1:46-55. We might think of Mary's song as the very first Advent hymn, and, as Bonhoeffer notes, "it is also the most passionate, the wildest, and one might almost say the most revolutionary Advent hymn that has ever been sung." It is, he adds, "a hard, strong, relentless hymn about the toppling of the thrones and the humiliation of the lords of this world, about the power of God and the powerlessness of humankind."

A heartwarming theme that arises from Bonhoeffer's sermon is how deeply God loves all those on the margins of society. "God draws near to the lowly, loving the lost, the unnoticed, the unremarkable, the excluded, the powerless and the broken. What people say is lost, God says is found; what people say is 'condemned,' God says is 'saved.'" Where people say No! God says Yes!"

Another theme is God's utter freedom to do as God pleases. Note how Bonhoeffer brings in those possessing humility of spirit: "only the humble believe and rejoice that God is so gloriously free, performing miracles where humanity despairs and glorifying that which is lowly and of no account."

A third theme (every sermon needs three points!) is the waiting, waiting, waiting of Mary. I consider how hard it is for me to experience "waiting expectantly" for the few weeks of Advent. For Mary it was nine months between the announcement by the angel that she was to be Mother of Messiah and the birth of the Christ child. Talk about "waiting expectantly"! I need to take my cue from Mary.

(((((FOURTH WEEK)))))

THAT SILENT NIGHT, THAT HOLY NIGHT

It's Christmas Eve. I have always found this night special, sacred even. I especially remember one Christmas Eve service when I was seven or eight. What I remember so vividly was the pastoral care of Eugene and Jean Coffin . . . "a pair of Jeans," as they liked to refer to themselves. They were *my* pastors.

Gathered worship was a studied experience in pastoral care and Eugene was especially gifted here. Of course, the focus of worship is always the triune Reality of Father, Son, and Holy Spirit. Eugene had an unusual ability in drawing us in close as the family of God. Once, years later, he explained to me that what he was seeking to do as the leader of worship was to be "baptized into a sense of the meeting." The phrase made immediate sense to me for I had experienced what he meant. The worship of God was a community experience, a family experience. Adoring. Worshiping. Praying. Listening. We were always urged to be aware of "the Presence in the midst." Even us kids learned to center down, be still, and listen to Christ our present Teacher.

That Christmas Eve service so many years ago was simple enough with Jean playing the organ and leading us in well-known Christmas carols. Then Eugene sat in a large rocking chair and gathered us kids at his feet. He scooped up a little child and sat her on his lap. In such settings children are often nervous and fidgety. But not this night. A holy hush seemed to cover us all, children and adults alike.

Eugene looked at us, each one individually, lovingly, quietly. Then he took out his Bible and read Luke's rendition of the Christmas story.

Like I say, the elements of the service were quite ordinary. No dimming lights. No flickering candles. None of the things that are supposed to create just the right mood. It wasn't the outward, physical things at all. It was the holy hush that fell upon us. It was "the Presence in the midst." It was the breaking in of the Shekinah of God. Even today, some seventy-two years later, I vividly remember that silent night, that holy night.

Utter, Stark Humility

It's Christmas Day . . . it is not hard to contemplate the subject of humility on this day. God, in Jesus bent down and became human like us . . . indeed, like one of the least of us. His mother was not yet married and her future husband had even contemplated refusing to marry her because of what seemed like an illegitimate pregnancy. Rejected at the inn they finally found a place for the birth of their baby, a "stable," a place for animals not people. Here in this place the birth of the Christ child occurred with no midwife to help. Following his birth Mary and Joseph placed the newborn Jesus in the only spot available, an animal feeding trough.

Utter, stark humility is the only way to describe the birth of the Savior of the world. And yet, heaven responded with an exuberant choir of angels singing, "Glory to God in the highest, and on earth peace, good will toward men" (Lk 2:14 KJV). I bow under the humility *and* the majesty of it all.

Prayerfully Reflecting on the Year Just Passing

Now is a good time to begin prayerfully reflecting on the year just passing. So . . .

What have I learned this past year about humility?

- I have learned that humility has been a prized virtue all through Christian history.
- I have learned that I can actually make progress in humility by cooperating with the grace of God.
- I have learned that humility makes me more human, more genuinely accessible to other people.
- I have learned that humility allows me to care more fully for the needs of others.

In this past year have I grown personally in the grace of humility?
This, I think, is a question others will need to answer, not me.
Okay, but does this mean that I cannot know anything about my own progress in humility?
Oh, no, not at all. I can, for example, reflect on some simple questions.

- Am I genuinely happy when someone else succeeds?
- Do I have less need to talk about my own accomplishments?
- Is the inner urge to control or manage others growing less and less in me?
- Can I genuinely enjoy a conversation without any need or even any desire to dominate what is being said?

Honestly considering these kinds of questions will help me know if the grace of humility is growing in me. And, if so, my response can be one of joyful thanksgiving to the God who is growing a grace in me that I could not do on my own.

What lessons can I take with me in the days ahead?

- I can be confident that humility is a virtue worthy of my best efforts.
- I can be confident that God is eager to grow the grace of humility in me.
- I can be confident that as I work in cooperation with God that my soul will grow in the grace of humility.

- I can be confident that the community of faith will be enriched as I mature in the virtue of humility.

NEW YEAR'S EVE—I LEAVE BEHIND MY LITTLE PRAYER

As this year draws to a close, I leave behind my little prayer that the Lord would . . .

- purify my heart,
- renew my mind,
- sanctify my imagination, and
- enlarge my soul.

I feel that praying in this simple way for the entire year has produced good fruit in my soul.

Still, I think the Lord wants to teach me more about praying. In one sense, I feel less sure of myself here than ever before. I want to learn "the prayer of the heart." But I sense I am not ready for such spiritual heights. No, I am sensing the Lord turning me back to the beginning, "Learn anew to love me . . . simply love me. Love me with all your heart, soul, mind, and strength."

So I shall . . . as best I can.

Finis

A CONCLUDING WORD

I began this journal study in humility because, everywhere I looked, I saw narcissism and greed and selfishness dominating the mood of our culture. This was a great sadness to me. It just seemed that people everywhere were at each other's throats.

But not completely. When I looked hard enough and long enough I could find individuals here and there who exhibited ordinary kindness and simple goodness. But they felt like isolated specks of light in a vast ocean of darkness.

So, I began to wonder about humility—this most fundamental of all virtues. For millennia humility has been valued as a rock-bed character trait of a good person. But not in our day. Why? And, what is humility anyway?

So I launched out into what in the beginning was mostly a personal search. I had been given a bright red journal book as a New Year's gift, and so I began my search by jotting odd notes and random reflections in it about this subject.

Along the way I have been exceedingly hesitant to say anything to anyone about my humility journaling project. Outside of Carolynn, our son Nathan was the first person I told.

I called him one winter afternoon to boast about our snow. (Now that he lives in Florida he has no need for his snowshoes!) The moment the words were out of my mouth I understood the reason for my hesitancy.

"Oh," Nate quipped, "a book on humility—that will make you famous for sure!" Smart aleck! His comment, of course, was double pronged. On the surface it was a joke about how few in our contemporary context would want to read about such a countercultural subject. But more deeply he was calling to my attention the incongruity of publishing a book on the subject of humility. "Humility," a virtue that focuses on obscurity and hiddenness; and "publishing," a business that stresses name recognition and a wide readership. I was struck with the contradiction. A bit of an oxymoron. To my surprise my search ultimately ended up as this book. Who could have imagined it?

This leads me to you, dear reader. You have picked up a book focused solely on the virtue of humility. You have chosen to reflect on a subject directly counter to the prevailing mood of our culture. Congratulations!

I hope your immersion into the subject of humility has caused you to move in humility's direction, even if ever so slightly. Do keep going. In due time it will lead you to a deep settledness in your spirit and a keen concern for the bruised and broken of our society.

So, I urge you, my reader friend . . .

- Be brave enough to learn humility.
- Be strong enough to learn humility.
- Be courageous enough to learn humility.
- Be compassionate enough to learn humility.

Acknowledgments

In my first book, *Celebration of Discipline,* I wrote, "Books are best written in community." I had no idea! The community now surrounding me is so much deeper and broader . . . I could never have imagined it. I cannot begin to express my debt to so many, both those living today and those who have passed through the Valley of the Shadow. But I will express gratitude where I can.

When I sought to imagine an authentic embodiment of the virtue of humility my mind took me way, way back to Bill and Irene Cathers. For many years Bill and Irene served Christ faithfully in Ecuador. Bill was the one who many years ago prayed for me, declaring prophetically, "I pray for the hands of a writer." Bill and Irene gave me a sustaining picture of humility in everyday life. I thank them.

I want to say a hearty thank you to Carolynn Foster, who stood by me all through my journal notations and reading and research, increasingly wondering with me if perhaps these ideas need to see the light of day in a book.

A special thank you goes to Nathan Foster. On numerous hikes in the Rockies we would discuss and debate and dream together, always seeking a clearer vision of "humility in daily life."

Then I want to express my thanks to a faithful group of readers who walked with me through the writing, offering counsel and insight: Mimi Dixon, Bob Fryling, Brenda Quinn, Lar Russell, and Pat Russell.

A large part of my rewrite work occurred down our country road five miles or so at Adriana's Restaurant. Adriana would graciously give me a quiet corner spot and always keep the coffee coming. So to Adriana and her staff—¡mil gracias!

Early in my writing career I might have concentrated on a writing project ten, twelve, sometimes fourteen hours straight. Now, in my eighties, I find my brain fried after only a few hours of concentration. So, once it became clear that this task was to become more than personal journal notations, I was concerned about how I might manage the research and copyediting and social media needed today for producing and launching a book. Right then three "superheroes" came to my aid.

Because I began this task simply by jotting observations in a journal, I had not taken the care to document sources for quotations. I mean, who footnotes observations in a journal? Of course, I had all the books, but finding so many obscure statements in so many books . . . ugh. It was here that Melody Leeper, a research person par excellence, came to my rescue. I would work with her for a few hours, whereupon my brain would be fried. But Melody kept at it ten, twelve, perhaps fourteen hours straight—"Sherlock Holmes sleuthing," she calls it. In the end she found every single reference. I thank her.

Next, if a book is to emerge, extensive work must proceed with a copyeditor. I cringed at the thought of such a myriad of technical details. Here my long-time friend and literary agent Kathy Helmers stepped in. Years ago Kathy and I had together written *Life With God* so she knew my writing style right down to the details of syntax. Graciously, Kathy volunteered to work with the copyeditor making the numerous decisions needed to produce a well-written book. I thank her.

Then, of course, a book project needs to find its way out into the public. In our day this demands extensive use of various online platforms. These are wonderful means of communication but I had some time ago made a decision not to engage in these forms of technology so I could focus my energies elsewhere. So Brian Morykon, director of communications for Renovaré, came to my rescue. Brian and the team at Renovaré have wonderfully agreed to help share widely the message of *Learning Humility,* and for this I thank them.

Finally, any substantive book project needs a strong publisher and a skilled editor. InterVarsity Press and Cindy Bunch, their divisional vice president and associate publisher, have fulfilled these roles wonderfully. Cindy oversees the Formatio line of books and has for years served as executive editor. Several years ago we started out on a project on a different subject, but after a couple years of researching forty-plus books on that topic I decided I had nothing of value to add. So, Cindy waited . . . and waited . . . and waited. And now, here we have *Learning Humility: A Year of Searching for a Vanishing Virtue.* I thank Cindy for waiting.

Further Reading

Below you will find some suggestions for reading on the virtue of humility. It is a brief list . . . I don't want to overwhelm you. Read what you find helpful and my guess is that these will lead you to other sources. I suggest you think of it as a grand treasure hunt into this most central of the Christian virtues. I list the books not alphabetically but as they appear historically. At the end I add a brief list of Lakota writings that I have found helpful.

The Holy Bible. Many editions and translations. The Bible is, without a doubt, the most important source we have for learning about humility. You might want to use several different translations along with a good concordance (I like *Young's Analytical Concordance to the Bible*). However, I suggest you not limit your study to passages using the word *humility*. For example, you might want to take one of the Gospels and see how many places the concept of humility is expressed in Jesus' action or teaching though the word is never used. You can do the same with the book of Proverbs. I am sure you will think of other ways to enhance your understanding of humility from Scripture.

Benedict of Nursia. *The Rule of St. Benedict in English*. Collegeville, MN: Liturgical, 1982. Benedict (c. 480–547) called this book "a little rule for beginners" and he sought to lay down "nothing harsh, nothing burdensome." As we know this small book launched the great Benedictine monastic tradition. Focus your attention on chapter seven where Benedict sets forth his "Twelve Steps into Humility." You might experiment with translating his thoughts on humility into the world in which you live.

Bernard of Clairvaux. *The Steps of Humility and Pride.* **Washington, DC: Cistercian, 1973.** Bernard (c. 1090–1153) wrote this book at the request of Godfrey of Langres, who had heard Bernard speak on humility and was hoping for some further guidance on the subject. However, Bernard felt that by experience he knew so much more about pride than he did about humility. So, Bernard gave something of a commentary on Benedict's steps up into humility and then contrasted them with parallel steps down into pride. He wrote, "Well, Brother Godfrey, you will, perhaps, complain that I have not given you exactly what you asked and what I promised. It looks as if I had described the steps of pride rather than those of humility. All I can say is that I can teach only what I know myself. . . . St. Benedict describes the steps of humility to you because he had them in his heart; I can only tell you what I know myself, the downward path. However, if you study this carefully you will find the way up." It makes for a fascinating read.

Thomas à Kempis. *The Imitation of Christ.* **Translated by William C. Creasy. Macon, GA: Mercer University Press, 1989.** Thomas à Kempis (c. 1380–1471) was part of the Brothers and Sisters of the Common Life, a lay movement which stressed the *Devotio Moderna,* or Modern Devotion. This was a renewal effort focused on bringing devotion into practical expressions like simplicity of life, humility of heart, and daily faith in Jesus. For half a millennium *The Imitation of Christ* has been the unchallenged devotional masterpiece for Christians everywhere.

The Cloud of Unknowing. **Translated by Carmen Acevedo Butcher. Boston: Shambhala, 2009.** Butcher, our translator, calls *The Cloud of Unknowing* (c. late 1300s) "a rainmaker for anyone whose soul has ever felt as dry as a bone." She continues, "Page after page our nameless author patiently explains what contemplative prayer is and how it can end any spiritual drought—shortages of love, low levels of humility, an absence of peace. Anonymous begins with a call to self-examination and humility, then recommends contemplative prayer as the only discipline that can deeply purify the soul" (ix). Here is a passage from *The Cloud* that I love: "I'm going to advise you to play a sort of game with God, seriously. Pretend you don't want what you want as much as you want it. . . . I'm confident that anyone with the grace to put my advice into practice will eventually experience the joy of God's playfulness. God will come to you, the way an earthly father plays with his child, kissing and hugging, making everything alright" (106).

Julian of Norwich. *Showings.* **Translated by Edmund College. The Classics of Western Spirituality. New York: Paulist, 1978.** Julian (c. 1343–sometime after 1416) was the first woman to write in the English language. Here is an example of her exuberant expressions: "God rejoices that he is our Father, and God rejoices the he is our Mother, and God rejoices that he is our true spouse, and that our soul is his beloved wife. And Christ rejoices that he is our brother, and Jesus rejoices that he is our savior. These are five great joys, as I understand, in which he wants us to rejoice, praising him, thanking him, loving him, endlessly blessing him, all who will be saved" (279).

William Law. *A Serious Call to a Devout and Holy Life.* **The Classics of Western Spirituality. New York: Paulist, 1978.** William Law (c. 1686–1761) was recognized as a master of the spiritual life as witnessed by persons as diverse as John Wesley, Samuel Johnson, John Henry Newman, Madame Guyon, and John Newton. For me one of his great contributions is his ability to help us see "devotion" not just as pious acts like prayer or various rituals but as "a life given or devoted to God." Law is not an easy read, but if you persevere you will be rewarded.

Andrew Murray. *Humility.* **Minneapolis: Bethany House, 2001.** Andrew Murray (c. 1828–1917) wrote voluminously on the spiritual life. He is one of only a scant few who has been willing to take on the task of writing directly on humility as "the first of the virtues, the best of all the graces and powers of the Spirit." Here is a lovely statement by Murray: "When we study the humility of Jesus as the very essence of His redemption, as the blessedness of the life of the Son of God, and as the virtue Jesus gives us if we are to have any part with Him, we will begin to comprehend how serious it is to lack humility in our lives" (34).

André Louf. *The Way of Humility.* **Translated by Lawrence S. Cunningham. Collegeville, MN: Liturgical, 2007.** André Louf (c. 1929–2010) goes directly to the ancient sources of the monastic tradition in order to help us think about humility. He quotes from a great variety of writers giving us a cornucopia of thought about this most central of the Christian virtues. These are his own words:

> One day, the *Apothegmata* tells us, Saint Anthony stepped out of his hermitage where he saw all the snares of the devil spread out like a net over the world. He let out a great groan of terror and cried out: "My God! How can anyone be saved?" A voice responded from heaven: "Humility." Consider that saying in the light of another one from the same Anthony: "Without temptations, no person can be saved." The conclusion is quite clear: As much as temptations are inevitable in the Christian life, they also clearly demand the practice of humility. (7)

The Way of Humility is well worth the time to read very, very slowly.

Rebecca Konyndyk DeYoung. *VainGlory: The Forgotten Vice.* **Grand Rapids, MI: Eerdmans, 2014.** In classical Christian thinking vainglory is a subset of pride and is perhaps *the* capital vice of modern culture. Rebecca DeYoung unravels for us the twisting paths of this most insidious of vices. She writes, "When we cut the onion of vainglory and confront its multiple layers, many of us might be unable to stop ourselves from crying—or at least despairing over making real progress against this vice. How can we break vainglory's hold when our lives are broadcast from a continuous feed of fathomless pride and fear?" (87). DeYoung then answers her own question by pointing us to the great Christian tradition of moral thinking and introduces us to the life-giving virtues, which alone can free us from the plague of narcissism that is the cultural zeitgeist of our day. A fascinating read.

SEVERAL LAKOTA WRITINGS

John G. Neihardt. *Black Elk Speaks.* **Spoken in Lakota by Black Elk. Translated by his son, Ben Black Elk. Written down in readable English by John G. Neihardt. New York: Simon & Schuster, 1959.** Heȟáka Sápa (1863–1950), known to us as Black Elk, was a famous holy man of the Oglala Lakota. He was second cousin to Chief Crazy Horse and participated in the Battle of Little Bighorn, which he describes as, "the rubbing out of Long Hair." At the age of nine Black Elk had his "Great Vision" in which he says, "I saw more than I can tell and understood more than I saw; for I was seeing in a sacred manner the shapes of all things in the spirit. . . . I saw that the sacred hoop of my people was one of many hoops that made one circle, wide as daylight and as starlight, and in the center grew one mighty flowering tree to shelter all the children of one mother and one father" (36). He did come into Christian faith while also continuing with his Lakota religious traditions.

Joseph M. Marshall III. *The Lakota Way: Stories and Lessons for Living.* **New York: Penguin Putnam, 2001.** Joseph Marshall III is Brulé Lakota, born and raised on the Rosebud Reservation. Though his first language is Lakota, all of his books are written in English. He is a superb storyteller and *The Lakota Way* is based on the twelve Lakota virtues: humility, perseverance, respect, honor, love, sacrifice, truth, compassion, bravery, fortitude, generosity, and wisdom. Marshall writes, "The virtues espoused by the stories in this book were and are the foundation and moral sustenance of Lakota culture. There is nothing more important. It isn't that we don't care about physical comfort or material possessions, it is because we don't measure ourselves or others by those things. We believe we are measured by how well, or how little, we manifest virtue in our life's journey" (xiii). *The Lakota Way* is an informative and delightful read.

Doug Good Feather. *Think Indigenous: Native American Spirituality for a Modern World.* **Carlsbad, CA: Hay House, 2021.** Doug (Wiyáka Wasté) Good Feather is full-blooded Lakota, born and raised in the traditional indigenous ways of his elders on the Standing Rock Reservation in South Dakota. He is a direct descendent of Chief Sitting Bull. He writes, "I was raised to be a warrior. But to be a warrior, I wasn't taught about war. I was taught about love, compassion, generosity, fortitude and courage. All of the things I needed to know and understand in order to take care of myself and be a warrior of peace and love" (ix). As you can tell he writes a lot about the Lakota virtues. A book to enjoy.

The Wisdom of the Native Americans. **Complied and edited by Kent Nerburn. Novato, CA: New World Library, 1999.** Kent Nerburn is one of the few American writers who can respectfully bridge the gap between Native and non-Native cultures. This collection of stories and quotes crosses over many Native American tribes and traditions. I am especially glad that Nerburn includes speeches from Chief Red Jacket, Chief Joseph, and Chief Seattle. Listen to this from Chief Luther Standing Bear of the Teton Sioux: "The Lakota was a true naturalist—a lover of Nature. He loved the earth and all things of the earth, and the attachment grew with age. The old people came literally to love the soil and they sat or reclined on the ground with a feeling of being close to a mothering power" (5). Nerburn has written sixteen books, so you might like to read several of his works, perhaps beginning with *Neither Wolf nor Dog: On Forgotten Roads with an Indian Elder.*

Pekka Hämäläinen, *Lakota America: A New History of Indigenous Power.* **New Haven, CT: Yale University Press, 2019.** Pekka Hämäläinen is obviously not Lakota. He is a Finnish scholar, presently the Rhodes Professor of American History at the University of Oxford. Be prepared for an extended scholarly discussion, but it is surprisingly readable. Listen to this: "In 1776 two nations were born in North America. One was conceived in Philadelphia, the other in the Black Hills of South Dakota, and they were separated by more than seventeen hundred miles. Exactly a century later those two nations would clash violently along the Little Bighorn River. . . . It was a collision between two radically different expanding powers that had conquered their way into the West, and its outcome was spectacular" (1). I encourage you to give this volume a try.

Notes

1. THE HARD MOON

8 *As I said before*: *The Cloud of Unknowing, with the Book of Privy Counsel*, trans. Carmen Acevedo Butcher (Boston: Shambala, 2009), 64.

9 *Humility is seeing yourself as you really are*: *The Cloud of Unknowing*, 36.

10 *Self-knowledge is the only way*: *The Cloud of Unknowing*, 39.
I will admit: *The Cloud of Unknowing*, 41.
The best way to grow in humility: *The Cloud of Unknowing*, 37.

11 *When by grace*: *The Cloud of Unknowing*, 40.
I . . . want you to be able to recognize: *The Cloud of Unknowing*, 40.

13 *I am reading an essay*: Rachel Donadio, "An Open Letter to Elena Ferrante —Whoever You Are," the *Atlantic*, December 2018, www.theatlantic.com /magazine/archive/2018/12/elena-ferrante-pseudonym/573952/.
Time like an ever-rolling stream: Isaac Watts, "O God Our Help in Ages Past" (1719), https://hymnary.org/text/our_god_our_help_in_ages_past_watts.

14 *Twelve Lakota virtues*: There is considerable discussion about the number of virtues. Some say four, some say seven, some say twelve. I am using the list from Joseph M. Marshall III, *The Lakota Way: Stories and Lessons for Living* (New York: Viking Compass, 2002).

2. THE MOON WHEN TREES CRACK FROM THE COLD

15 *The first and most important step*: "12 Lakota Virtues, Essential to Balance and Happiness," White Wolf Pack, November 2014, www.whitewolfpack .com/2014/11/12-lakota-virtues-essential-to-balance.html.

18 *The Greek view of humility*: Gerhard Kittel, "*tapeinos*," in *Theological Dictionary of the New Testament*, 10 vols. (Grand Rapids, MI: Eerdmans, 1977).
The mother and mistress of all the virtues: Cited in André Louf, *The Way of Humility*, trans. Lawrence Cunningham, Monastic Wisdom Series 11 (Collegeville, MN: Liturgical, 2007), 6.
Humility comes from elsewhere: Cited in Louf, *The Way of Humility*, 7.

21 *Twelve steps of humility*: Benedict of Nursia, *The Rule of St. Benedict in English*, ed. Timothy Fry (Collegeville, MN: Liturgical, 1982), 32-38.

3. THE MOON OF THE SORE EYES

25 *In spite of difficulties we persist*: "12 Lakota Virtues, Essential to Balance and Happiness," White Wolf Pack, November 2014, www.whitewolfpack .com/2014/11/12-lakota-virtues-essential-to-balance.html.

30   *These thoughts draw me*: Dallas Willard, *The Disappearance of Moral Knowledge* (New York: Routledge, 2018).

31   *The vision was of the six sacred directions*: John Neihardt, *Black Elk Speaks* (New York: Pocket Books, 1972), 40.

32   *Do not imagine*: C. S. Lewis, *Mere Christianity* (New York: MacMillan, 1952), 99.

35   *My sacrifice is a contrite spirit*: John Michael Talbot, "Come to the Quiet," *Come to the Quiet*, Sparrow, 1980.

36   *the board felt*: David Rooks, "Breaking: Black Elk Peak Soars Above the He Sapa, No Longer Harney Peak," *Indian Country Today*, August 12, 2016.
      I was standing on the highest mountain: Neihardt, *Black Elk Speaks*, 36.

4. The Moon When the Ducks Come Back

39   *A basic teaching among all tribes*: "12 Lakota Virtues, Essential to Balance and Happiness," White Wolf Pack, November 2014, www.whitewolfpack .com/2014/11/12-lakota-virtues-essential-to-balance.html.

42   *Humility is a virtue*: Bernard of Clairvaux, *The Steps of Humility & Pride* (Trappist, KY: Cistercian, 1973), 30.

43   *A more ripe and rank case*: US Supreme Court, *United States vs. Sioux Nation of Indians*, 448, US 371 (1980), https://supreme.justia.com/cases /federal/us/448/371/.
      The Lakotas were awarded $105 million: Fred Barbash and Peter Elkind, "Sioux Win $105 Million," *Washington Post*, July 1, 1980, www.washington post.com/archive/politics/1980/07/01/sioux-win-105-million/a595cc88 -36c6-49b9-be4f-6ea3c2a8fa06/.
      We don't think of the air and water: Frederic. J. Frommer, "Sioux Hold Out for Land's Return," *Seacoast Online*, August 19, 2001, www.seacoastonline .com/story/news/2001/08/19/sioux-hold-out-for-land/51294880007/.
      All of our origin stories: Steve Young, "A Broken Treaty Haunts the Black Hills," June 27, 2001, https://lakotadakotanakotanation.org/BrokenTreaty HauntsBLACKHILLS.html.

45   *reach the highest summit*: Benedict of Nursia, *The Rule of St. Benedict in English*, ed. Timothy Fry (Collegeville, MN: Liturgical, 1982), 32.

50   *The tenth step of humility*: Benedict of Nursia, *Rule of St. Benedict*, 37.
      At times he simply cannot: Bernard of Clairvaux, *The Steps of Humility*, 68.

51   *I'd rather be jolly St. Francis*: Thomas R. Kelly, *A Testament of Devotion* (New York: Harper & Row, 1941), 92.
      I had doubts about my own ability: Bernard of Clairvaux, *The Steps of Humility*, 28.

52   *Well, you may perhaps say*: Bernard of Clairvaux, *The Steps of Humility*, 82.

5. The Moon of Making Fat

55   *Being honorable means*: "12 Lakota Virtues, Essential to Balance and Hap-
     piness," White Wolf Pack, November 2014, www.whitewolfpack.com/2014
     /11/12-lakota-virtues-essential-to-balance.html.

56   *This moon is named for female animals*: "Thirteen Lakota Moons," Aktá
     Lakota Museum & Cultural Center, http://aktalakota.stjo.org/site/News2
     ?page=NewsArticle&id=8911.

59   *The eight godly virtues*: Evagrius of Pontus, cited in Richard Foster and
     Gayle Beebe, *Longing for God: Seven Paths of Christian Devotion* (Downers
     Grove, IL: InterVarsity Press, 2009), 54-64.

60   *There is one vice*: C. S. Lewis, *Mere Christianity* (New York: MacMillan,
     1952), 94.

     I have found an essay: Grace Hamman, "Julian of Norwich's Children:
     Childhood and Meekness in *A Revelation of Love*," *Journal of Medieval
     and Early Modern Studies* 49, no. 1 (January 2019).

61   *As truly as God is our Father*: Julian of Norwich, *Showings* (New York:
     Paulist, 1978), 295-96.

     Julian's similitude of the mother and child: Hamman, "Julian of Nor-
     wich's Children."

62   *The Sweet gracious hands*: Julian of Norwich, *Showings*, 302.

     The humility and meekness: Julian of Norwich, *Showings*, 300.

6. The Moon of the Green Leaves

66   *It does not require many words*: From Joseph's speech at Lincoln Hall,
     Washington, DC, 1879. Joseph's Nez Perce name is *Hin-mah-too-yah-lat-
     kekht*, "Thunder rolling over the mountains."

     More than just compassion: "12 Lakota Virtues, Essential to Balance and
     Happiness," White Wolf Pack, November 2014, www.whitewolfpack
     .com/2014/11/12-lakota-virtues-essential-to-balance.html.

68   *Despite such international recognition*: Paul Brand and Philip Yancey, *Fear-
     fully and Wonderfully: The Marvel of Bearing God's Image* (Downers Grove,
     IL: InterVarsity Press, 2019), 2.

69   *I can imagine God*: Brand and Yancey, *Fearfully and Wonderfully*, 6.

     Assurance that the Christian life: Brand and Yancey, *Fearfully and Wonder-
     fully*, 6.

70   *God doth not need*: John Milton, "Sonnet 19: When I Consider How My
     Light Is Spent," Poetry Foundation, www.poetryfoundation.org/poems
     /44750/sonnet-19-when-i-consider-how-my-light-is-spent.

70 *Pride is the cause*: Evagrius of Pontus, cited in Richard Foster and Gayle Beebe, *Longing for God: Seven Paths of Christian Devotion* (Downers Grove, IL: InterVarsity Press, 2009), 60.

71 *My words and thoughts*: George Herbert, "Colossians 3:3: Our Life Is Hid with Christ in God," in *The Temple: Poetry of George Herbert* (Brewster, MA: Paraclete, 2001), 81.

72 *For the Lakota there was no wilderness*: Kent Nerburn, *The Wisdom of the Native Americans* (Novato, CA: New World Library, 1999), 5.

74 *The first and most essential element*: Andrew Murray, *Humility: The Journey Toward Holiness* (Minneapolis: Bethany House, 2001), 39.

75 *He [Jesus] says, "Do not blame yourself*: Julian of Norwich, *Enfolded in Love: Daily Readings with Julian of Norwich* (Minneapolis: Seabury, 1980), 49.

7. The Moon When the Berries Are Good

79 *Sacrifice is giving of oneself*: "12 Lakota Virtues, Essential to Balance and Happiness," White Wolf Pack, November 2014, www.whitewolfpack .com/2014/11/12-lakota-virtues-essential-to-balance.html.

82 *Tranquility, gentleness, and strength*: Evelyn Underhill, *Essential Writings* (Ossining, NY: Orbis, 2003), 39-41.

83 *The pain and tension which must be felt*: Underhill, *Essential Writings*, 39-41.
    Means effort, faithfulness, courage: Underhill, *Essential Writings*, 39-41.

84 *The fruits of holy obedience*: Thomas R. Kelly, *A Testament of Devotion* (New York: Harper & Row, 1941), 61.

85 *Humility and holiness are twins*: Kelly, *A Testament of Devotion*, 67.
    Prone to wander: "Come, Thou Fount of Every Blessing," lyrics by Robert Robinson, 1758, https://hymnary.org/text/come_thou_fount_of_every_blessing.
    Growth in humility is a measure: Kelly, *A Testament of Devotion*, 63.
    O how slick: Kelly, *A Testament of Devotion*, 62.
    Only the utterly humble: Kelly, *A Testament of Devotion*, 64.
    More, they who see God: Kelly, *A Testament of Devotion*, 65.
    I am continuing to read: Jeffrey Ostler, *The Lakotas and the Black Hills: The Struggle for Sacred Ground* (New York: Penguin, 2011).

86 *In a vision quest*: Sparrow Hart, "What Is a Vision Quest?" www.sparrow hart.com/what-is-a-vision-quest/.

87 *O God of earth and altar*: G. K. Chesterton, "A Hymn: O God of Earth and Altar," The Society of G. K. Chesterton, www.chesterton.org/a-hymn-o -god-of-earth-and-altar/.

89 *The larger book*: Pekka Hämäläinen, *Lakota America: A New History of Indigenous Power* (New Haven, CT: Yale University Press, 2019).

89 *The smaller volume*: Joseph M. Marshall III, *The Lakota Way: Stories and Lessons for Living* (New York: Viking Compass, 2002).

8. THE MOON WHEN THE CHOKECHERRIES ARE BLACK

91 *Truth is being honest*: "12 Lakota Virtues, Essential to Balance and Happiness," White Wolf Pack, November 2014, www.whitewolfpack.com /2014/11/12-lakota-virtues-essential-to-balance.html.

92 *I asked my grandfather once*: Joseph M. Marshall III, *The Lakota Way: Stories and Lessons for Living* (New York: Viking Compass, 2002), 119.

We Lakota have heard Iktómi: Marshall, *The Lakota Way*, 121.

Established the Great Sioux Reservation: Marshall, *The Lakota Way*, 121.

94 *No Moccasins*: Marshall, *The Lakota Way*, 1-8.

95 *One night it was cold and rainy*: Marshall, *The Lakota Way*, 5.

96 *I have known good people*: Marshall, *The Lakota Way*, 7.

The burden of humility: Marshall, *The Lakota Way*, 19.

Jesus doesn't use his power: Noah Van Niel, "Manly Virtues: Can Masculinity Be Good?" *Plough Quarterly*, Winter 2021, 96-97.

98 *The fact that others know*: Thomas à Kempis, *The Imitation of Christ*, trans. William C. Creasy (Macon, GA: Mercer University Press, 1989), 37.

99 *The Christian man*: W. S. Bruce, *The Formation of Christian Character: A Contribution to Christian Ethics* (Edinburgh: T&T Clark, 1908), 6.

I hope to yet be like him: Bruce, *The Formation of Christian Character*, 7.

Ethics receives: Bruce, *The Formation of Christian Character*, 7.

101 *Life demands that we exercise perseverance*: Marshall, *The Lakota Way*, 202.

102 *Lastly, courage and bravery*: William Law, *A Serious Call to a Devout and Holy Life* (Louisville, KY: Westminster John Knox, 1955), 350-51.

Let every day . . . be a day: Law, *A Serious Call*, 259.

9. THE MOON OF THE HARVEST

103 *Doing what is right in caring*: "12 Lakota Virtues, Essential to Balance and Happiness," White Wolf Pack, November 2014, www.whitewolfpack .com/2014/11/12-lakota-virtues-essential-to-balance.html.

104 *Come thou Fount of every blessing*: "Come, Thou Fount of Every Blessing," lyrics by Robert Robinson, 1758, https://hymnary.org/text/come_thou _fount_of_every_blessing.

105 *You do not become a contemplative overnight*: Paula Hurston, *The Hermits of Big Sur* (Collegeville, MN: Liturgical, 2021), 4.

107 *Humility does not rest*: Thomas R. Kelly, *A Testament of Devotion* (New York: Harper & Row, 1941), 62.

107 *Humility rests on a holy-blindedness*: Kelly, *A Testament of Devotion*, 62.
Growth in humility is a measure: Kelly, *A Testament of Devotion*, 63.

110 *I have seen in our midsummer*: Kent Nerburn, ed., *The Wisdom of the Native Americans* (Novato, CA: New World Library, 1999), 93-94.
She [Clare] embodied Christian truth: Wendy Murray, "On Her Deathbed, Clare of Assisi Blessed God," *Christian Century*, July 21, 2021, www.christian century.org/article/reflection/her-deathbed-st-clare-assisi-blessed-god.
Poverty is a noose: Native American Inspirational Quotes, "Sioux Proverb: Poverty Is a Noose That . . . ," https://howtoliveonpurpose.com/8049/founders/native-americans/native-american-inspirational-quotes-poverty-is-a-noose-that/.

10. THE MOON OF THE BROWN LEAVES

117 *Bravery is born*: "12 Lakota Virtues, Essential to Balance and Happiness," White Wolf Pack, November 2014, www.whitewolfpack.com/2014/11/12-lakota-virtues-essential-to-balance.html.

118 *Hail, Queen Wisdom*: John Michael Talbot, "The Praises of the Virtues," *Troubadour of the Great King* (Sparrow Records, 1998).
The Litany of Humility: "A Christian Litany of Humility," attributed to Rafael Cardinal Merry del Val, "Humility Prayers," free online resource at JesuitResource.org, www.xavier.edu/jesuitresource/online-resources/prayer-index/humility, accessed May 16, 2022.

120 *For the litany composed by Cardinal Merry*: C. S. Lewis to Don Giovanni Calabria, March 27, 1948, *Collected Letters of C. S. Lewis*, vol. 2 (New York: HarperCollins, 2004).

121 *Ohiyesa, "The Winner"*: "Dr. Charles A. Eastman Ohiyesa (The Winner): Santee Sioux," Aktá Lakota Museum & Cultural Center, http://aktalakota.stjo.org/site/News2?page=NewsArticle&id=8884. Excerpted from the biographical notes at the end of *The Essential Charles Eastman (Ohiyesa)* (World Wisdom, 2007).

122 *We know that all religious aspiration*: Kent Nerburn, *The Wisdom of the Native Americans* (Novato, CA: New World Library, 1999), 83.
branded us: Nerburn, *The Wisdom of the Native Americans*, 83.
In these matters I wish to express my debt to Dr. Dallas Willard, especially his unpublished notes in "Studies in the Book of Apostolic Acts: Journey into the Spiritual Unknown."

125 *We first Americans mingle*: Nerburn, *The Wisdom of the Native Americans*, 83.
Prayer—the daily recognition: Nerburn, *The Wisdom of the Native Americans*, 90-92.

126 *There was undoubtedly much*: Nerburn, *The Wisdom of the Native Americans*, 127.

11. The Moon When the Wind Shakes Off the Leaves

129 *After learning patience*: "12 Lakota Virtues, Essential to Balance and Happiness," White Wolf Pack, November 2014, www.whitewolfpack.com /2014/11/12-lakota-virtues-essential-to-balance.html.

130 *Humility and holiness are twins*: Thomas R. Kelly, *A Testament of Devotion* (New York: Harper & Row, 1941), 67.

133 *I saw that an humble man*: John Woolman, *The Journal of John Woolman and a Plea for the Poor*, John Greenleaf Whittier Edition Text (Secaucus, NJ: Citadel, 1972), 18.

136 *Quotations from Thomas Aquinas, Thomas à Kempis, Bernard, and Augustine*: Andrew Murray, *Humility: The Journey Toward Holiness* (Minneapolis, MN: Bethany House, 2001), 21, 51, 59, 89.

137 *Humility is the only soil*: Murray, *Humility*, 17.
I had long known the Lord: Murray, *Humility*, 18.
Let us at the very outset: Murray, *Humility*, 18.
The pride Satan breathed: Murray, *Humility*, 45.

138 *Nothing sets a person*: Jonathan Edwards, quoted in Murray, *Humility*, 58.
I will here give you: Murray, *Humility*, 104-5.

12. The Moon of the Rutting Deer

140 *'To have a heart'*: "12 Lakota Virtues, Essential to Balance and Happiness," White Wolf Pack, November 2014, www.whitewolfpack.com/2014/11/12 -lakota-virtues-essential-to-balance.html.

141 *But through the revelation*: John Woolman, *The Journal and Major Essays of John Woolman*, ed. Phillips. P. Moulton (Richmond, VA: Friends United, 1989), 19.
The untold story of the Lakotas: Pekka Hämäläinen, *Lakota America: A New History of Indigenous Power* (New Haven , CT: Yale University Press, 2019), 3.

142 *The most improbable expansion*: Hämäläinen, *Lakota America*, 3. This remarkable work of history is fascinating reading, if a bit hefty at 530 pages.

143 *Only to sit and think of God*: "My God, How Wonderful Thou Art," lyrics by Frederick Faber (1849), https://library.timelesstruths.org/music/My _God_How_Wonderful_Thou_Art/.

144 *The essential vice*: C. S. Lewis, *Mere Christianity* (New York: MacMillan, 1952), 94.

146   *Humility, rooted in an accurate*: Catherine J. Wright, *Spiritual Practices of Jesus: Learning Simplicity, Humility, and Prayer with Luke's Earliest Readers* (Downers Grove, IL: IVP Academic, 2020).

148   *All the saints are convinced*: François Fénelon, *Christian Perfection* (New York: Harper & Brothers, 1947), 205.

150   *Dee Brown's fine book*: Dee Brown, *Bury My Heart at Wounded Knee* (New York: Picador, 2007).

151   *Black Elk's report on Wounded Knee*: John Neihardt, *Black Elk Speaks* (New York: Pocket Books, 1972), 217-23, 230.

13. The Moon When the Deer Shed Their Antlers

154   *Only after one has learned*: "12 Lakota Virtues, Essential to Balance and Happiness," White Wolf Pack, November 2014, www.whitewolfpack .com/2014/11/12-lakota-virtues-essential-to-balance.html.

156   *On Jordan's bank the Baptist's cry*: "On Jordan's Bank the Baptist's Cry," lyrics by Charles Coffin, https://hymnary.org/text/on_jordans_bank_the _baptists_cry.

157   *The Great Spirit Prayer*: "The Great Spirit Prayer," trans. Chief Yellow Lark, Atka Lakota Museum and Cultural Center, http://aktalakota.stjo.org/site /News2?page=NewsArticle&id=8580.

159   *As I plod along my brain is fixated*: I am well aware of the 1973 siege and occupation of Wounded Knee by the Oglala Sioux and the American Indian Movement's (AIM) armed defiance. The results were mixed. It did attract wide media coverage to the plight of the Lakota people. But it failed to accomplish its key goal of removing Tribal President Richard Wilson, who was accused of enormous corruption and abuse. Several died in the struggle, most importantly Buddy Lamont, who was well-known in the Pine Ridge tribal family. The occupation lasted for seventy-one days and ended May 8 following Lamont's death.

   Lakotas will endure: Pekka Hämäläinen, *Lakota America: A New History of Indigenous Power* (New Haven, CT: Yale University Press, 2019), 392.

160   *It is also the most passionate*: Dietrich Bonhoeffer, "My Spirit Rejoices," *The Collected Sermons of Dietrich Bonhoeffer*, ed. Isabel Best (Minneapolis: Augsburg Fortress, 2012), 115.

   God draws near to the lowly: Bonhoeffer, "My Spirit Rejoices," 118.

   Only the humble believe: Bonhoeffer, "My Spirit Rejoices," 120.

Also by Richard J. Foster

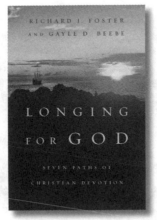

Longing for God
978-0-8308-4615-3

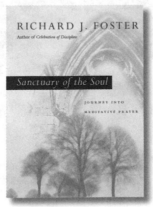

Sanctuary of the Soul
978-0-8308-3558-4

Renovaré